"Those who bring their big q l
find a stimulating guide to thi

—**DOROTHY BASS**, author of Receiving the Day, and
Valparaiso Project on the Education and Formation of People in Faith

"Accessible and engaging, Anthony Siegrist speaks of God
in ways that invite readers from all walks of life into life-
giving conversation."

—**DEBRA DEAN MURPHY**, associate professor of religious studies at
West Virginia Wesleyan College and author of *Happiness, Health, and
Beauty*

"Anthony Siegrist makes theology come alive. When you finish
this book, your mind will be dancing with new words and ideas
about faith and God."

—**CAROL PENNER**, assistant professor of theological studies at Conrad
Grebel University College

"Anthony Siegrist writes with clarity and ease, and his theology
is generous, winsome, and deep. I am often asked to recommend
books to people new to theological thinking. Siegrist's work has
shot to the top of my list."

—**STEPHEN BACKHOUSE**, dean of theology for the local church at
Westminster Theological Centre, director of Tent Theology, and
author of *Zondervan Essential Companion to Christian History* and
Kierkegaard: A Single Life

"Anthony Siegrist serves as a trustworthy and wise guide who is
not afraid to tackle tough questions. His definitions, examples,
and life stories leap from the page to the intersection of faith
and life."

—**JONI SANCKEN**, associate professor of homiletics at United Theological Seminary

SPEAKING
of GOD

SPEAKING
of GOD

{ An Essential Guide
to Christian Thought }

ANTHONY G. SIEGRIST

HERALD
P R E S S

Harrisonburg, Virginia

Herald Press
PO Box 866, Harrisonburg, Virginia 22803
www.HeraldPress.com

Library of Congress Cataloging-in-Publication Data
Names: Siegrist, Anthony G., 1979- author.
Title: Speaking of God : an essential guide to Christian thought / Anthony
   G Siegrist.
Description: Harrisonburg : Herald Press, 2019. | Includes bibliographical
   references and index.
Identifiers: LCCN 2019011004 | ISBN 9781513806068 (pbk. : alk. paper) |
   ISBN 9781513806075 (hardcover : alk. paper)
Subjects: LCSH: Theology.
Classification: LCC BR118 .S526 2019 | DDC 230--dc23
LC record available at https://lccn.loc.gov/2019011004

SPEAKING OF GOD
© 2019 by Herald Press, Harrisonburg, Virginia 22803. 800-245-7894.
   All rights reserved.
Library of Congress Control Number: 2019011004
International Standard Book Number: 978-1-5138-0606-8 (paperback);
   978-1-5138-0607-5 (hardcover); 978-1-5138-0608-2 (ebook)
Printed in United States of America
Cover and interior design by Reuben Graham

Unless otherwise noted, Scripture text is quoted, with permission, from the *New Revised Standard Version*, © 1989, Division of Christian Education of the National Council of Churches of Christ in the United States of America.

23 22 21 20 19   10 9 8 7 6 5 4 3 2 1

To those who have taught the faith in the only way it can be—
with modesty, courage, and a little humor

May the words of my mouth and the meditations of all of our hearts be acceptable in your sight, oh Lord, our rock and our redeemer.

—A preacher's prayer based on Psalm 19:14

CONTENTS

1

GETTING STARTED

I feel sometimes as if I were a child who opens its eyes on the world once and sees amazing things it will never know any names for and then has to close its eyes again.
—**John Ames, in *Gilead* by Marilynne Robinson**

Theology, at its most basic level, is nothing more than speaking together about God. It is an ongoing conversation, one that can intrigue us and draw us in. Whether we're new to the discussion or have been involved in it for a lifetime, theology should be immersive and transformative. It should bring us joy.

I was in high school when I first encountered a really intriguing idea about God. It wasn't the first conversation I had on the subject of God; far from it. I was involved in a Christian youth group and attended church. We talked about God, along with politics and sports, in the home where I grew up. But I can remember the morning when I first got the sense that this was all far bigger and far deeper than I had been led to believe.

My Bible class met on the first floor of my Christian high school, near the administrative offices. All the Bible classes met in rooms at that end of the school. We were surrounded by paper timelines of the Protestant Reformation, and had the sense that the administrators were listening through the hall door. The Reformation was the point in the sixteenth century when the church in the West broke apart—or as our teachers told the story, it was the point when the church got its act together, with our spiritual ancestors leading the way.

We were mindful of the proximity of the administrators when our teachers struggled to manage discussions about God and sex. On that particular morning, the teacher had drifted into some of the ideas that had been hot topics when he was in seminary. My sense was that he hadn't prepared for class and was buying time until the bell rang. I was doodling in my notebook when he mentioned the name Karl Barth (1886–1968). Barth believed that the Bible wasn't God's Word in itself, our teacher said, but that it *became* God's Word as we read it and as the Spirit enlivened it. That doesn't quite do justice to Barth's view of Scripture, but what mattered then was that I hadn't heard that idea before—and that my teacher's professors had thought the idea quite scandalous.

I was hooked. Could it be that the reading and study of Scripture meant more than trying to dig up whatever it was the author had meant? Could it be that thinking and intellectual work were spiritual activities? Could it be that the Spirit didn't just move when worship music was blaring?

I was intrigued but not particularly driven. It wasn't until the idea had bumped around in my head for a few days and I found myself in the library with no pressing assignments that I finally searched the stacks for something by Karl Barth. I found a slim volume with his name on the spine. The final *h* in his last name surprised me; it wasn't how my teacher had pronounced it. The book hadn't been checked out in years. I puzzled over it for an hour and left it in the library. Slim as that book was, I couldn't make out what the Swiss theologian was going on about, and I couldn't uncover even a trace of the potent ideas my teacher had described.

That was about twenty years ago—twenty years of books, conversations, and postsecondary degrees. I think I'm now officially a seasoned theology nut. But the ideas still excite me. I know that this is not everyone's experience. Some people's introduction to theology is more like my uncle's introduction to lakes in northern Ontario. I was a boy of three or four when I went down to the lake to watch my extended family return from fishing. I remember seeing my uncle, a stout middle-aged man, sitting in the stern of a canoe pulled halfway out of the water. He sat there with a fishing rod in one hand and a paddle in the other. He lurched forward ever so slightly, getting ready to climb out of the canoe. Then it tipped. He flailed for something solid to grab, and finding nothing, flipped over like meat on a spit. The cold water and knee-deep muck made him gasp and sputter. As far as I know, he never regained trust in canoes, lake bottoms, or my other uncle, who should have been steadying the canoe. He couldn't shake the worry that one wrong move might dump him once more into the drink. Beginning to study theology is sometimes like that. It can feel forced and ungrounded, and can leave us without any desire to try again.

One of the reasons theology can be intimidating is that theologians tend to have a lot to say. One of the best examples is the Italian theologian Thomas Aquinas (1225–74). For centuries a rumor persisted that Thomas could levitate. That probably was not true, but it is true that his writings fill a shelf by themselves. Early in Thomas's life, when he first expressed his intention to join the Dominican monastic order and become a theologian, his brothers tried to change his plans by hiring a woman to seduce him. Legend says that Thomas overreacted a bit and chased her

away with a fire iron. Later, while studying in Paris, he was bul-
lied by classmates and called a "dumb ox." That seems to have
been an overreaction on the part of his classmates. Thomas is one
of the most important theologians of the medieval period. He
claims that theology is primarily about God, but he also points
out that since God is the origin of everything, just about anything
can find a place in a theological discussion.[1] This gave him quite
a bit to write about.

It has been a while since I was bested by that little Barth volume. Since then I have published a couple of academic books,
but they would barely fill a soap tray. I certainly can't levitate,
but I have spent quite a bit of time helping people find their way
around the Christian faith. This involves not only explaining the
relevant vocabulary and history but also listening to conversations about faith and the big questions of life: How do we know
if we are living well? How should we respond to the beauty we
encounter every day? What about the pain and the ugliness?
These are conversations about God and the implications of divinity; they are theological conversations. I'm sure that you have
had conversations like these as well. If you have, it means your
feet have already been in theological waters. These discussions
are lively and deeply meaningful. When we consider theology in
more formal ways, we are simply adding a level of care and organization to the talk about God we're already doing.

Like any conversation, theology involves both speaking and
listening; it involves discerning together what is true and what
is good and what is beautiful. The challenge is that any good
discussion requires a shared language. We live in a time when
we have access to more information than previous generations,
yet many of us are not as familiar with the people, concepts, and
history of the Christian community as we would like to be. This
makes participation challenging. It also means that our talk about
Scripture and the Christian life is regularly reduced to emotivism

("I feel this . . .") or Bible-thumping ("This verse says that . . ."). We're also easily influenced by teachers and movements that have the same features of the shows we watch—slick graphics, heart-warming endings, or us-against-them posturing. We quickly lose the overwhelming sense of beauty that our talk about God ought to provoke. We crumple the mystery of the divine into the havoc of partisan politics.

Our lack of biblical and theological literacy means that our churches are having a hard time finding well-prepared lay leaders and that our ability to respond with faithfulness and creativity to large-scale cultural shifts is seriously hampered. Not long ago I found myself waiting for lunch beside a well-traveled church consultant and ordained Baptist minister. She assured me that these challenges are widespread. "It isn't just that our communities don't like change," she said; "it's that we don't quite know what direction change should take us." Many of our churches are flummoxed by the appearance in their midst of various bits and pieces of our global technological society. At a time when our broader culture seems to be going a hundred ways at once, it's important that Christian communities nurture their ability to speak about God, about Scripture, and about our lives with care and attention.

Theology is a serious conversation, but it's also implicitly humorous. We are, after all, trying to speak with precision about things like God and the origin of our own existence. We should be willing to laugh at ourselves. That being the case, theology still doesn't lend itself well to short attention spans or little blurby statements. If our fast-paced global culture is being consistently reminded of anything, it's that things of value take time to develop. In 2007, Carlo Petrini, the founder of the Slow Food movement, met the Prince of Wales. The Slow Food movement started in Italy (no surprise there) as a way of resisting the development of a fast-food franchise near Rome's Spanish Steps. The British newspaper

The Guardian featured an article about the meeting between Petrini and the British prince. It began this way: "Not since Jesus rustled up a feast from some fishes and a few loaves of bread . . . have we invested food with such spiritual qualities; and if food has become the faith of a decadent West, its high priest is Carlo Petrini. When the founder of the Slow Food Movement met the Prince of Wales last week it was hard to say who was having the audience."[2]

Petrini's message was that we should eat better—probably less as well, but certainly better. And "better" means slower. By now the term *slow* has been used to positively describe all kinds of things, but I want to suggest that it could be used to describe a good theological conversation. Slow theology is the product of careful attention and maturity. Learning to participate—or even better, to *contribute*—takes time. Fast food is fine if you want to fuel yourself the way you would fuel a car, but if you want something deep, a bit more refined and timeless, then you need to invest some focused attention.

A FORECAST

I don't know if you've ever had someone tape a sporting event so you could watch it later. You probably told them not to tell you who won. Not knowing the outcome is what makes watching something like that the most engaging. In other situations, though, it's good to know the general outline of the story so you can dig into the details.

Here is where this book is going. Think of it first as a little introductory handbook on Christian theology. The ancients would have called it an *enchiridion*, which means the same thing. Early in the sixteenth century, a Dutch scholar named Erasmus (1466–1536) wrote a little book known in English as the *Handbook of a Christian Knight*. He was trying to convince the friend of a friend that being a Christian required him to act like Christ, not just do some rituals. The English translation runs a little over one hundred pages. Many years before, Augustine of Hippo (354–430) wrote a little book usually called *The Enchiridion of Augustine*. Augustine was a reformed partier who admitted that in his youth he stole fruit and had too many lovers. Augustine and Erasmus are towering figures. My only connection to them as an author is that I think they were on to something when it comes to the need for handbooks. If you've got the gumption, read one of theirs instead of this. You should know, though, that Augustine's handbook contains 122 chapters. This one only has 18—though, to be fair, his chapters are shorter.

In writing this book I've learned how hard it is to make a slim introduction. It's difficult to know what details are essential, like which of the many important figures I should mention. It's also difficult to know when to share personal bias. One of the first introductory theology books I read was by C. S. Lewis (1898–1963). Aside from a few peripheral moments like my encounter with Karl Barth, I didn't get into much theology as a high school student. It wasn't until several years later that I took another shot at something that sounded vaguely like a theology book. I was in Trinidad as a community volunteer assisting a church when I picked up a book by C. S. Lewis. Lewis was a scholar of classical languages and literature. I found a copy of his *Mere Christianity* in a church library in a little town that straddled the island's main highway. Lewis's clear prose and easy way of unfolding complex arguments drew me in. *Mere Christianity* was probably the first theology book I took seriously. I had read quite a bit before that, mostly novels, some biographies, and the panoply of books assigned at school. One summer when I broke my ankle I even skimmed my parent's entire encyclopedia set. Yet there was something about the ideas Lewis opened up that I found more alluring. They seemed to matter.

I still have a deep respect for Lewis's book, but one thing I've learned since is that there is no such thing as "mere" Christianity.

There is no generic way to introduce this subject. Even attempting to use "unbiased" scientific and historical tools would do nothing more than give us an introduction with a certain type of bias. Learning to speak about God demands both courage and humility: courage because generic statements just won't do; humility because our perspective is just that, our perspective. If we're going to talk about God, we must own our words.

This can all be a little frustrating. Sometimes we just want to be told "the way things are." We don't want to mess with sorting various branches of the Christian family tree. The problem, though, is that "the way things are" is always the way you or I *think* they are. It's the way we *see* things. This doesn't mean objective reality doesn't exist, just that we only have particular accounts of it, accounts shaded by human culture and our own experiences.

In *Speaking of God*, my intention is to be conscious of the variety of ways Christians see things but also to deliberately cross many of the traditional boundaries between Christian groups. To make my own biases a little more transparent, I will tell you more about myself here and throughout the book. In addition to studying and publishing, as I've mentioned already, it's worth knowing that I pastor a Protestant church, more specifically a Mennonite church, in Canada's capital city. Being Mennonite means that our congregation traces its roots to Radical Reformers of the sixteenth century. These Reformers, known as Anabaptists, were unique in that they didn't think matters of faith should be enforced with violence. This is my current church home, but I've also worshiped and studied with Anglicans for nearly a decade. I taught at an evangelical college for almost the same amount of time. There are things I love about each of these communities and things that frustrate me.

Whatever our backgrounds might be, when we join the theological conversation we join a discussion that is well underway.

So while we can't speak about God generically, we can look to those who have come before to see how they have sorted the central issues from the peripheral ones. Just because most Christians agree on some things, like the divinity of Jesus and the triune character of God, doesn't necessarily make the traditional perspective true. It does mean, however, that we should be careful about making off-the-cuff changes. In this book I'll try to encourage us to honor traditional wisdom while remembering that a central assumption of Christianity is that we should be open to change—something we call repentance.

Like any book, this one has been influenced by a host of voices. I draw from a long list of scholars and pilgrims. As a pastor-theologian, I've become especially taken with ancient Christian thinkers who worked before the intellectual universe was chopped up into so many different fields of study. They moved with grace between what we would now think of as Christian doctrine, biblical studies, philosophy, psychology, rhetoric, and even, in some cases, math and the natural sciences. They were less concerned about being experts in one particular thing than they were with pulling it all together into a way of being that had integrity.

One of my working assumptions is that the Christian community needs people who can link things together. We need people with hybrid identities who can connect the rest of us. I've spoken to lots of people who understand their faith in a hybrid way, a blend of the charismatic movement and Eastern Orthodoxy, for example. I know Anglican-Anabaptists. Hybridity is messy, but these sorts of fusion identities represent the future of Christianity. Younger Christians are inclined to see the strengths of various denominations and to identify themselves first as pilgrims in the ancient way of Jesus and only secondarily with particular subgroups or denominational tribes. If you're a Christian who thinks your particular home group has everything figured out, or if you think true Christianity begins and ends with your denomination, then the pages that follow—and the future of the church—will require a great deal of your patience.

I've organized this book according to the canonical structure of Scripture. The **biblical canon** is the list of texts, or books, contained in the Bible. Working with this order means that we start with the Old Testament—more specifically, with the first five books of the Bible, which are also known as the Torah—and continue on through the New Testament, ending with the pastoral letters and the book of Revelation. I think this structure, which makes this book different from most introductory theological volumes, is a natural way to pursue our subject, and I've found it useful in the classroom. What's more, many classical theologians taught theology in direct relationship to Scripture.

Since I've ordered things this way, we should note a couple of things early on. First, the canonical order isn't the same as the standard order of philosophical or systematic theology. This displaces some of the questions that we might wish were dealt with earlier rather than later. If you work your way through to the end, however, we'll have covered most of the basics. Second, the canonical order roughly follows the sweep of history. That seems sane enough. Yet this can give the impression that the beginning is somehow more important than the end. In Scripture, the key definition of the central character—God—comes into focus in the life and work of Jesus. I'll give that part of the plot away right here. This part of the story, though, comes near the end. For that reason, we must look at some things about Jesus before we turn to the Old Testament. We'll get to those in the next chapter. Nevertheless, most of this book is shaped by biblical and historical contours, the story of God's redemptive interaction with humanity, and the story of the community that understands its own existence as encircled by the biblical narrative.

Throughout the book, key theological terms are printed in boldface and the lifespans of significant pre-twentieth-century theologians are given in parentheses. However, if you want to explore a particular topic or theologian further you'll need to consult a dictionary of theology. You should know, too, that some historical events are hard to date with precision. Many I've given here are the educated guesses of historians. Throughout the book, I tell a little more of my own story. Not all the events I recount occurred precisely in the order they appear here.

In all of this—the larger architecture and the details—I hope this book helps you join the conversation about being a faithful and imaginative follower of Jesus. Conversations like these— whether we have them in class, in a church basement, beside a campfire, or on a long drive—are valuable for their own sake. Through these conversations, we figure out what we believe, what sort of lives we want to cultivate, and what we might hope for in the future. As Thomas Aquinas suggested, they get us into everything. That's certainly how it's been for me.

2

A **WILD OLIVE SHOOT**

A People with a Story

Theology that puts a handle to the power of God is no longer a theology but a demonic theological ideology. Theology must refuse to "handle" the saving power of God.
—**Kosuke Koyama**

People, even Christian people, are sometimes skeptical that theological words and concepts are necessary at all. I encountered that perspective after beginning to read theological literature. The mission agency that facilitated my experience in Trinidad wasn't keen on heady stuff. For them, the Christian faith was as much about emotion as about anything else. Education and critical thinking, the leaders said, got in the way of connecting personally with God.

I did not find this convincing. The faith I knew then had too many holes. Too much randomness. Too many questions. After returning from Trinidad, I decided to set aside my plans to study science at a university and to enroll in a small theological college instead. I wanted to study more about Scripture and to join the Christian tradition's long conversation about God.

Remembering this kind of skepticism about theology—that it could get in the way of experiencing God—prompts me now to begin some of my presentations on the subject with two photos. The first shows a table prepared for a feast—Thanksgiving maybe, or Christmas. There is a lot of food, a beautiful centerpiece, and carefully laid place settings. The second photo shows a grubby hand clutching a paper cup with some loose change inside. I ask participants which of the two images they would like to symbolize their future.

Of course it's not a realistic question. We all want to imagine that we will be prosperous. I ask the question to set participants up for another pair of images. Since Christian theology is anchored in the Scriptures, I share two passages from the book of Jeremiah. One is a well-known verse: "For surely I know the plans I have for you, says the LORD, plans for your welfare and not for harm, to give you a future with hope" (Jeremiah 29:11). The second passage is less celebrated; part of it reads: "Therefore thus says the LORD: I am going to send you off the face of the earth. Within this year you will be dead" (Jeremiah 28:16).

Many of us have found comfort in the first passage, which assures us that God has plans for us and will protect our futures. Who doesn't want hope and a future? Fewer of us are familiar with the second passage, and fewer still want it to apply to ourselves.

So now I ask the group a real question, one with a bite: "Why is it that we apply the first passage to our lives and not the second?" Many of the people I speak to have read a significant amount of the Bible and consider themselves committed to the faith. Even so, few can explain why the first passage should apply to their lives and not the second. And few can explain how the *you* in either passage relates to them at all. This gets us thinking. If Jeremiah wasn't addressing me as a twenty-first-century Christian, how can I read this passage? On the other hand, if his words *do* have something to say to you and me, what might it be?

DOORWAYS AND DEAD ENDS

Scripture has had a profound effect on many people. Consider Dietrich Bonhoeffer. Bonhoeffer came from a very cultured and highly educated family in Berlin. He became an important church leader and theologian during World War II. Bonhoeffer was arrested by the Nazi government and was hanged at a concentration camp just before the end of the war. Much of his remarkable life was put in motion by an experience in his mid-twenties. He described what happened to him to a friend named Elizabeth Zinn:

> I came to the Bible for the first time. It is terribly difficult for me to say that. I had already preached several times, had seen a lot of the church, had given speeches about it and written about it—but I still had not become a Christian, I was very much an untamed child, my own master. I know, at that time I had turned this whole business about Jesus Christ into an advantage for myself, a kind of crazy vanity. . . . It was from this that the Bible—especially the Sermon on the Mount—freed me. Since then everything is different. I am clearly aware of it myself; and even those around me have noticed it. That was a *grand liberation*. . . . I now saw that everything depended on the renewal of the church and of the ministry. . . . Christian pacifism, which I had previously fought against with passion, all at once seemed perfectly obvious. And so it went further, step by step. I saw and thought of nothing else. . . . My calling is quite clear to me. What God will make of it I do not know. . . . I must follow the path.[1]

For Bonhoeffer, reading the Bible with openness and humility led to a sense of meaning and identity. Of course this didn't only happen to him. Augustine, the North African theologian whom we've already met briefly, was in a crisis of belief when he heard a child's voice chanting, "Tolle lege" (Pick up and read). Obeying changed his life. Martin Luther (1483–1546) was the ignition charge of the Protestant Reformation. Years earlier he was a spiritually confused young man, a monk obsessed with his sense of guilt. He read Romans 1:17 and it was a moment of revelation. There are countless less famous and more disturbing examples as well, including Vernon Wayne Howell's transformation when his attention was drawn to Isaiah 34. We'll get to that story shortly.

Careful listening to Scripture can give us a sense of what it means to live our lives well. It can help us speak about the big picture. It can free us from simply going through life without a sense of what's important. If we don't have a clear sense of what makes our life meaningful, then tech companies and fashion magazines will convince us of their vision. Yet the simple truth is that few Christians can clearly describe how the Bible connects with their lives. Part of what made the Scriptures transformative for people like Bonhoeffer and Luther were the assumptions they made about this connection.

In the absence of knowing how to make this connection, many of us have opted for a sentimental approach like the one I encountered in my volunteer experience before college. This way of reading is driven by our self-interested, emotional instincts. Something applies to us because we *want* it to: "What this passage means to me is ____." We often choose our preachers and teachers the same way. We listen to those who affirm what we already think. This has us skating on thin ice.

Or if emotional expressions of faith aren't our thing, we might just do our best to listen to people who are "biblical." By "biblical" we probably mean someone who quotes the Bible a lot. If we stop and think about it, however, this ice isn't very thick either. Consider this: Near the end of May 1637, some Puritan settlers in New England massacred several hundred defenseless Indigenous villagers, mostly women, children, and elderly men. They justified their actions by appealing to Judges 20 and 2 Samuel 12.[2] It sounds as if they thought their actions were biblical. Quoting the Bible a lot doesn't make a book or a speaker any more Christian than hitting lots of balls in random directions makes someone a golfer. Direction matters.

We might take a slightly more sophisticated approach, one in which we view the Bible as a collection of facts or commands that all have equal value. I encountered this in my first year as a theology student. It seemed scholarly at first. In this perspective we think of reading the Bible a bit like conducting a poll or looking at research data plotted on a graph. When we want to know the biblical view of something—say, how many wives someone should have—we look up every reference to the topic and go with whatever position gets the most votes. This is essentially what people do who develop grand spiritual theories based on "word studies."

Some of us get so desperate for divine direction that we treat the Bible as if it's magical. Maybe we can't figure out how to fix our hair. Perhaps this dilemma seems like the end of our life, so we let the Bible fall open and point to a verse. Luckily, our finger lands on Leviticus 10:6 or 1 Corinthians 11:14 instead of Ezekiel 5:1. Sometimes God meets us despite ourselves. The problem comes when we turn these happy incidents into a universal method.

What we're talking about here is **hermeneutics**, or how we discern what a text means. Everyone who reads the Bible has a hermeneutical approach even if they can't explain it in technical terms. The truth is, we can't avoid hermeneutical questions when it comes to reading any text and considering its significance for our lives. That's especially true of the Bible. But perhaps you're thinking something like, "Don't we just need to pay attention to a passage's context?" or "Can't I just pray about a passage to figure out what God is saying to me?" Well, maybe.

Let's say archaeologists found the autobiography of the apostle Paul hidden in some crypt beneath the city of Rome. Maybe Paul wrote it when he was in prison. This would be fantastic! It would answer lots of questions, like what Paul meant when he referred to his "thorn," and whether he was married. However, would knowing all this do much for *our* lives? God *may* have told an ancient moon-worshiping nomad (to pick on Abraham) to leave his home in modern-day Iraq. God *may* have told a group of tribes to wander around in the Negev desert. So what? How is anything God reportedly did or said to them relevant to you or me? Even if we could know exactly what ancient Israel thought the first chapters of Genesis meant, what does that mean to us? How does the Bible have universal relevance? Knowing more about the ancient authors doesn't answer these questions.

BOTTLES IN THE OCEAN

Earlier, I mentioned a man named Vernon Wayne Howell, whose life was changed by reading Isaiah 34. The phrase from Isaiah that caught Howell's attention was one of the middle lines from verse 16: "none shall be without its mate." Howell had fallen in love with a young woman, and this line gave him the courage to follow the tradition of the time and approach her father. Her father was not at all in favor of the relationship, and he happened to be a leader in the congregation that Howell attended. The young man got the boot. Later, Howell connected with a related community known as the Branch Davidians.

In 1990, Vernon Wayne Howell successfully petitioned a judge, "for publicity and business purposes," to change his name to resemble the ancient Persian king Cyrus, or as it is sometimes transliterated, Kurosh. In 1993, David Koresh, claiming to be reestablishing the Davidic kingdom, was confronted by government agents. He died in the violence, as did dozens of his followers, including some children.

David Koresh knew the Bible. Malcolm Gladwell, famous for books like *Blink* and *The Tipping Point*, says that with respect to knowing the Bible, Koresh was "without peer."[3] Yet most of us would say Koresh got it wrong. Very wrong. Yet I wonder how many of us could say *why* his hermeneutical approach—his way of connecting Scripture to his life—was mistaken. Did he not pray for divine illumination? Did he fail to think the book was important enough? Where did he go wrong?

Theology is about bringing some intentionality and purpose to this connection between Scripture and our lives. It is about gaining the tools to see how passages like Jeremiah 29:11 *and* Jeremiah 28:16 apply to us. In one sense this is a very old path. An ancient Christian would have had a long period of learning and formation before joining the church. In another sense this learning is always fresh and new. Lamin Sanneh, who was a professor at Yale Divinity School, pointed out that one of the unique features of Christianity is that it is transmitted without using the language of its founder.[4] The language Jesus spoke (Aramaic) isn't even the language of the Gospels (Greek). Learning to take part in the theological conversation requires us to learn to read the Bible well *and* to learn to speak truthfully about God in new contexts.

When I say these sorts of things in public, someone will inevitably tell a story about a person they know who had a very different experience. It might be a story about someone who found a Bible in a hotel room and was transformed by reading John's gospel. The meaning of the Bible, the critic says, is obvious. If only we could convince folks to read it, everything would be all right. My response is to say that someone, somewhere, has also probably met their spouse by putting a note in a bottle and chucking it into the ocean. We can be happy for them but still not be confused about best practices for finding a marriage partner. For Christians across the globe, theological training has proven essential for reading the Bible well. It's only that, as the contemporary theologian Ellen Charry says, "theology is not just an intellectual art"; it's a way of cultivating "the skill of living well."[5]

STRANGERS AT THE DOOR

Let's imagine that the Bible is an apartment building. It contains stairs, hallways, and a warren of rooms. How do we find our way around? What's our way in? Here we must recognize, again, that the authors of the biblical texts weren't writing directly to us. New Testament or Old Testament—none of the authors had us in mind. So how do we get in? Attempting to read Scripture as if it were a collection of timeless, objective statements or trying to read it in light of our own idiosyncratic experience—that's a bit like climbing ladders or fire escapes that might take us up the side of the building, to the roof maybe, or at best into one room through a window. But it doesn't take us in through the front door. One of the first theological moves we need to make is simply to pause and reflect on how it is that we enter this foreign text.

If you've been reading Scripture for a while, you know that in the New Testament, ethnicity means something quite different from what it does in the previous part. Paul says in his letter to the Galatians that "there is no longer Jew or Greek, there is no longer slave or free, there is no longer male and female; for all of you are one in Christ Jesus" (Galatians 3:28). This is an important clue. Somewhere in the biblical story, something fundamental shifts. And it happens in the second chapter of Acts during a celebration called Pentecost. Pentecost was an annual Jewish festival commemorating God's giving of the law on Mount Sinai. Its modern equivalent is known as the Feast of Weeks. In Acts we hear about one particular celebration of this festival, which occurred just after Jesus' ascension.

Jesus' followers were gathered together in Jerusalem. Suddenly they heard the sound of wind and saw a tongue of fire resting on each person. Luke, the author of Acts, says that the disciples began to speak in other languages. This drew a crowd of people who wanted an explanation. So Peter did what he had been taught to do: he looked to Scripture. If he hadn't said anything, the crowd would have run with their first theory—that the babblers had too much to drink. The mental catalog of Scripture that Peter flipped through would have been what we call the Old Testament. Sometimes we call it the Hebrew Scriptures or even the First Testament, to not make it sound so obsolete.

Peter found a connection in the words of the prophet Joel and told the crowd that what they were observing was the fulfillment of something anticipated long ago. He quoted from the second chapter of Joel: "Then afterward I will pour out my spirit on all flesh; your sons and your daughters shall prophesy, your old men shall dream dreams, and your young men shall see visions. Even on the male and female slaves, in those days, I will pour out my spirit" (vv. 28-29).

Joel was speaking of an extension of Israel's story into a different kind of future. Peter, then, made the connection to the events unfolding around him. What we don't always notice is that the link Peter saw is not obvious. Here's how Peter put it later in Acts 2: "This Jesus God raised up, and of that all of us are witnesses. Being therefore exalted at the right hand of God, and having received from the Father the promise of the Holy Spirit, he has poured out this that you both see and hear" (vv. 32-33). Peter referred to the Father, to Jesus the Son, and to the Holy Spirit, what later Christians would come to call the Holy Trinity. However, it's the presence of Jesus in history that ignites the whole explosion, reshaping what it means to be a part of God's people and changing who gets to claim the Scriptures as "their" mail. Jesus changed things.

When God's Spirit is at work, the status quo is never left unchallenged. There are lots of examples. In the mid-twentieth century, the people at Koinonia Farm in Sumter County, in the U.S. state of Georgia, challenged the normalcy of racial segregation. They got more attention than they probably wanted. Some of the attention was violent. *Koinonia* is a Greek word that shows up in Acts 2. It's translated as "fellowship" in verse 42 and as "common" in verse 44. The members of Koinonia Farm believed that God had initiated a better way of relating to each other. If Jew and Gentile had been brought together as one people in Christ, then other racial boundaries also needed to be overcome.

Two millennia after Pentecost, each of us is still being welcomed into the people of God. In Romans 11, Paul uses the metaphor of a new limb being grafted onto an older tree. If we combine this with the observation from Lamin Sanneh—about translating the words of Jesus—we get a strong hint, even an elbow to the ribs, about the ongoing global welcome that is the Christian faith. Sanneh writes, "The new conception of religion as fixed in no revealed language or single culture and as bound by no exclusive geographical frontier but rather as truth abiding with believers, whoever and wherever they happened to be, was constitutive of the identity of Christianity as mission from the very beginning."[6] This fundamental embrace of cultural and ethnic variety is the place where non-Jews are taken into the heart of the biblical story.

It's only when we pause and allow the Bible to become a little strange—to become the property of others—that we see the beautifully wide embrace of the early faith. When we understand that this embrace occurs through Jesus, we begin to read Scripture in a *Christian* way.

Jesus is the door that gives us access to the big, rambling building that is the Bible. It makes more sense when we enter through his life, his death, and his resurrection. We can use all kinds of other metaphors to make this point: Jesus Christ is the center, the key, the foundation, the vine, the lens. Each of these underlines how we should engage the Bible. The theological term for reading the Bible with Jesus as our access point is **Christocentrism**.

This hermeneutic follows the lead of early Christians. Contemporary theologian J. Todd Billings observes that this is the way people in the New Testament read the Hebrew Scriptures. Billings says, "In appropriating the Hebrew Scriptures christologically, the New Testament writers did not restrict the meaning of the Old Testament to something like the author's original intentions, or to how the Old Testament text would have originally been heard."[7] The New Testament writers believed that the event of Jesus Christ shed light on the older Scriptures, revealing the substance they had foreshadowed.

Obviously, not everyone was convinced by Peter's sermon. Yet his claim wasn't a one-off. The beginning of Hebrews 8 makes basically the same point. The author says that things like sacrifices, the priesthood, and other features of ancient Israel's worship were rough copies; they were shadows of true, heavenly things. Christians believe that Jesus Christ gives these ancient pointers to God more clarity and dimension.

The language we use to speak of God as revealed in Scripture is shaped by our acknowledgment of Jesus as the door through which we enter the warren of Scripture. It is this mode of reading that separates saints from cult leaders. What some of us learned in Sunday school or catechism or from TV preachers wasn't all wrong: the right answer is almost always "Jesus." A Christian biblical hermeneutic begins with a person, a living person—Jesus Christ.

3

In the BEGINNING

Seeing the World

The first word of the Bible has hardly for a moment surfaced before us, before the waves frantically rush in upon it again and cover it with wreaths of foam. That the Bible should speak of the beginning provokes the world, provokes us. For we cannot speak of the beginning.
—**Dietrich Bonhoeffer**

My choice of theological colleges was guided by what should have been a secondary factor. As much as I wanted to study theology, I also wanted to learn to rock climb and kayak. I was fortunate not to have to choose between these. I found an academic program that would allow me to spend time in the mountain ranges that span the U.S.-Canada border. The world-famous Banff National Park was only a couple of hours away from the college's library. Banff is Canada's oldest national park, and should you ever find yourself on this continent with a few weeks to burn, it is a wonderful destination for a road trip. The mountains of northwestern Montana are some of the wildest areas in the United States. Spending time in wilderness landscapes has always been a spiritual experience for me. As I met others in these places, at trailheads and visitors centers and conferences, I learned that it wasn't just me. Sensing something of the divine in these places is common. Yet I also learned that a visceral response to natural beauty doesn't lead us all to the same conclusions.

Imagine some theologically curious visitor observing a place like Banff in the spring. She might notice the massive hanging glaciers atop the park's broad-shouldered peaks, and she might see the meltwater spill over the edge of an alpine pond and flash in the evening light as it plunges hundreds of meters in a showy rush. It's not hard to imagine this visitor concluding that there is something beyond our universe, something she might call God—Something or Someone who is glorious, massive, beautiful, sustaining, and constant. She might go on to believe that God has a wonderful plan for her life, a plan that will be carried out with the determination of a glacier shaping a valley floor.

What if the visit doesn't end there, though? What if the next morning the theological pilgrim happily hikes through a high meadow and pauses to watch some young bighorn sheep leap from rock to rock? She imagines they're as gleeful as children on summer break. The belief that God loves her and wants her to kick up her metaphorical heels is just beginning to flood the hiker's soul when a shadow passes. She looks up to see a golden eagle tuck its wings and drop. In a show of force, the bird grabs a formerly happy sheep in its talons, cranks its wings, and lumbers away. What now is our park visitor to think? The rest of her visit is marred by the knowledge that nature is, as Alfred, Lord

Tennyson, says, "red in tooth and claw."[1] She can't help but wonder if the capricious eagle, deliverer of death from the sky, also points to God.

THE STRUCTURE OF THINGS

We arrive at the first book of the Bible, the book of Genesis, as readers who have been connected to it through the ministry of Jesus. It has meaning for us because Jesus has made us part of the people who claim this book as their own. What we find here is a text that helps us see the cosmos. It helps us see how we relate to whoever or whatever stands beyond it. It's important to recognize that Genesis isn't the only part of the Bible that talks about the origin of things. Several texts produced by the Pentecost community—passages that are now in our New Testament—tell us that God created the world through Jesus the Anointed One. I'm thinking of verses from the opening chapters of the gospel of John and from the letters of Hebrews and Colossians. John refers to Jesus as the Word of God, or we might say, as the logic of the universe. The world we encounter bears the fingerprints of the Word.

Genesis itself begins with this: "In the beginning when God created . . ." That phrase sets out the essential structure of how Christians see things. It asserts what one wouldn't necessarily glean from observing the world. We're talking here about what philosophers call **metaphysics**, the basic structure of existence. There is God, and then there is creation. One is prior and independent, the other follows and is contingent. Whatever happens next—the creation of humans or the advent of evil—happens within this basic frame of Creator and creation. This seems basic, but to speak of things this way is already to see the world in a particular fashion. It is different from seeing the world itself as God or from thinking that the universe we know arises out of nothing and has no meaning or value beyond itself.

Tennyson's description of nature's violence comes from a long poem he published in 1850 to commemorate a friend who died of a brain hemorrhage. The friend died just before he was to be married. Nine years later, in unrelated circumstances, the naturalist Charles Darwin published *On the Origin of Species*. Darwin observed that natural selection, in which the fittest survive, explains the diversity of life. The observations of Tennyson and Darwin push toward us questions about this earth we call home. We wonder about the basic character of things. Are there causes at work beyond the physical mechanics described by science? We wonder about the meaning of beauty and suffering. Why, we wonder, should we think that God is more like a caring physician than a serial killer?

To ask these kinds of questions—to talk about how we see the universe and whatever might be beyond or beneath it—is one of the most profound theological discussions we can have. An Austrian engineering-student-turned-philosopher, Ludwig Wittgenstein (1889–1951), referred to the famous duck-rabbit image to make a point about seeing. You have probably seen the image: it's the drawing that can seem to be showing either a duck looking left or a rabbit looking right.[2] The world is similar. It can be seen in several ways, depending on the presuppositions we bring to the moment of observation. This means that "seeing" is never just seeing, but always seeing in a particular way. This is as true for Christians as it is for Muslims, Buddhists, and atheists. The beginning of Genesis is about how to see things.

GOD AND THE WORLD

The Christian Scriptures don't always speak with one voice. Some of the Bible's authors were prophets, some were kings, some lived in cities, some lived in villages, some were colonized, and some were more like colonizers. The writers had a range of views on their own political situations. For instance, try to figure out whether ancient Israel's desire for a king was a good thing. The authors are diverse, yes, but they are not without common convictions. At a very general level we observe that the biblical authors share a way of seeing the world shaped by the assumption that there is something bigger and beyond. They believe that Something or Someone transcends the physical stuff they can see and touch. This mysterious, **transcendent** One isn't quite a thing and isn't quite a creature. The imprecision in our language here is because all the words we use, even in theological conversations, refer to stuff within the created world. That said, the idea of transcendence isn't unique to the Bible.

In 2004, a pitcher for the Boston Red Sox, Curt Schilling, pitched the sixth game of the American League Championship Series with a tendon in his ankle held in place by sutures. Blood seeped from the wound during the game. The Red Sox won. Schilling's bloody sock became famous. We say his effort was "worth it" because it contributed to something that transcended his injury: his team's mission to win a trophy. Transcendence, even in smallish things like sports, is something we assume. It can't be measured or poked or prodded. We're trained to interpret individual events within a bigger story. Going for a run—what is just placing one foot after another in a controlled fall—has meaning because it relates to a runner's goal of training for a climb or losing a few pounds. We might say that a police officer killed on duty was valiant because he or she sacrificed for the greater good. This is all part of how we see things.

A basic assumption that envelops Christian ways of seeing the world is that this transcendent Something isn't merely an idea in our heads or an inert thing. It is an active being, a being that creates, and in turn a being that reveals the deep things, the things that stand behind and underneath the cosmos. This means that God isn't just an object we study, but an agent, an acting subject. So we say that God is not only transcendent but also **immanent:**

God is relational and engaging. In the opening chapters of Genesis we read that God creates and then communicates to creation: God calls it all "very good" and then gives the human creatures a position of responsibility within it.

Simon Chan, a Singaporean theologian trained at Cambridge, emphasizes the importance of describing God in both these ways. He writes, "The traditional doctrine of immanence *and* transcendence carries a number of important spiritual implications. . . . It implies that God is both relational . . . [and] it implies the freedom of God, the idea that creation and redemption are the free acts of God." Chan points out that although many Western Christians place more emphasis on God's immanence, other Christians in parts of the world more conscious of social upheaval and exploitation place greater value on divine transcendence. God's existence beyond the chaos of life gives them hope.[3] But because God isn't just a transcendent object, because God is relational and revelatory, the authors and editors of Genesis assume we can know some things about God. We also know things about our world and about ourselves that are beyond the scope of scientific observation.

God's self-communication in Genesis foreshadows God's self-communication in Jesus. It's a basic characteristic of the biblical God: God speaks. One phrase repeated throughout the creation story is "And God said . . ." Sometimes we're in such a rush to have this part of the Bible answer our questions about how or when life came to be that we miss the emphasis on God's speech. The speech, or the word of God, is the answer to the classic question, Why is there *something* rather than *nothing*? This means that as we encounter the world, we inevitably encounter God's speech. God's speech creates, and God's speech reveals. Theologians have traditionally spoken of two ways in which this divine communication, or revelation, takes place. One of these ways we call **general revelation**. This refers to God's rudimentary self-disclosure through the world around us. It's the sort of thing a Banff visitor could be thinking about. It's what happens when we are entranced by the beauty of the world and experience a sense of awe and reverence.

The sixteenth-century reformer John Calvin (1509–64) said that general revelation gives us all an "awareness of divinity." Calvin's intellectual legacy is known as the Reformed tradition. One of my college teachers was an avid fan of Calvin. He told us of how when he was a student he once rode around the city twice because he forgot to get off the bus. He was reading Calvin's famous *Institutes of the Christian Religion*. One of the things Calvin believed was that there has never been even a single household without some sort of religion.[4] Simply by being alive and aware we sense that there is something more than the material world. We sense that we are more than the firing of neurons and compartmentalized saline solution. And we sense that the *more* of us connects in some way with the *more* of the cosmos.

General revelation also gives us a sense that life involves oughts. Not everyone agrees on what we *ought* to do, but we all have a sense that we should do certain things even if they violate our desires in the moment. For Calvin, and for most other theologians, the general awareness of transcendence and *oughtness* isn't specific or powerful enough to fix our problems. Yet it is one way of explaining the significant overlap between the world's great faiths. It also suggests that Christians should affirm the existence of truth in other religions, in science, and in thoughtful people generally.

One of the things I'll always remember about going to college on the edge of the prairies was driving under the open skies. The little college town where I lived was just close enough to the mountains that we could see them from the empty western end of the main street. If we left town for the day and returned after dark, we would often see a string of several dozen lights on the horizon. They would blink on and off: red sparks against the black sky. They weren't directed at us specifically; anyone driving across that part of the prairies could see them. They didn't change when we got closer. They didn't stop when we crossed the railroad tracks and entered town. Even when we went inside, those lights kept blinking, marking the locations of giant wind turbines. That's how we can think of general revelation. It doesn't compel us, but it continually orients our world, however vaguely, to justice and a semblance of order. It suggests there is something more.

DISRUPTIVE REVELATION

The second way in which God's speech reveals is not at all like the blinking lights of general revelation, those basic cues nature gives us about God's existence and the character of life. **Special revelation** is the way we speak about God's direct self-disclosure. You have to be there to get it. General revelation is constant; special revelation is disruptive and unique. This is the message God speaks into a specific situation through divine messengers like prophets or angels, or through Scripture, or through the church or—most significantly—the speech of God that takes on flesh: Jesus of Nazareth.

On December 26, 2004, one corner of God's creation—the floor of the Indian Ocean off the western coast of northern Sumatra—was shaken by a magnitude nine earthquake. Waves less than a meter high in the open ocean sped toward shorelines at the speed of a commercial jet. As the waves slowed in shallower water, some grew to more than ten meters. Crashing ashore, the tsunami killed over two hundred thousand people in more than a dozen countries. Nearly two million were left homeless.

Along with the rush to provide aid were the questions, chiefly this one: Where was God? This is hardly a new question, but it was particularly poignant in the early days of 2005. There was the video footage of the destruction, so nobody could deny how horrible it was. There was also the reality that nobody can be blamed for an earthquake. Many journalists offered their thoughts. Some said that this finally showed there could be no such thing as a loving God. The Eastern Orthodox theologian David Bentley Hart later wrote that some of these writers decided to announce that at long last, "the materialist creed has been vindicated: that here we have an instance of empirical horrors too vast to be reconciled with belief in a loving and omnipotent God, and that upon this rock the ship of faith must surely founder and sink and leave nothing but fragments of flotsam to wash up into the shoals of the future."[5] Hart wasn't at all impressed with the hasty conclusions of these commentators. He thought they were naïve.

A little book called *The Doors of the Sea* was Hart's response. In it Hart showed how the idea that terrible events could disprove God's existence was founded on a view of God that dismissed special revelation. It was a view of God created by rationalist observation. This kind of thing is not much help in understanding the difference between faith and naiveté or pointless pain and valuable struggle. Only special revelation can tell us enough about divinity to speak to the way God relates to a world that includes horrific pain. Only special revelation can speak to a God whose Word takes on flesh.

CREATURES OF DUST

The first chapter of Genesis ends with the Creator's declaration that "it was very good." As the biblical story moves on, connecting more clearly with the world we know, things are disrupted and overturned. God's basic assessment of creation never wavers, though: it is very good. And at that, Genesis tells us, God rested. God settled into place with the whole earth as a temple. This is the climax of the Bible's opening story—God's ceasing work and settling into place.

Since the time of Tennyson and Darwin, it has been hard to talk about these early chapters of Scripture without thinking about how they might relate to evolutionary science. On one side are folks who believe that Adam and Eve existed, that their children had sex with each other, and that the earth is only about six thousand years old. On the other are those who think all life evolved from a bubbling of primordial soup, that humans descended from monkeys, and that the Bible can't be trusted.

Of course this description isn't fair to either side or to the multitudes in between. But each side tends to describe the other with extremes. Years after my initiation into theological studies and mountain rambles, I experienced this lack of understanding firsthand. This Genesis stuff can be touchy business.

As a college student, I doubt I would have done much with the suggestion I'm about to give here. I was inclined then to see things in oppositional terms and to see people I disagreed with as problems. Now I'm inclined to follow Augustine's advice. Augustine did have a tumultuous youth, but it wasn't ten years after he became a Christian and returned to North Africa that he was ordained a priest and then a bishop. His wisdom was obvious. He began preaching and writing, and writing and preaching. He wrote something like a three-hundred-page book every year ... for forty years. In a book he never finished, called *The Literal Meaning of Genesis*, Augustine reminds his readers that non-Christians know a lot about how natural things work. So he worries about "reckless and incompetent expounders of Holy Scripture" giving the wrong impression about the Bible. He continues:

> It is a disgraceful and dangerous thing for an infidel to hear a Christian, presumably giving the meaning of Holy Scripture, talking nonsense on these topics; and we should take all means to prevent such an embarrassing situation, in which people show up vast ignorance in a Christian and laugh it to scorn. The shame is not so much that an ignorant individual is

derided, but that people outside the household of faith think our sacred writers held such opinions, and, to the great loss of those for whose salvation we toil, the writers of our Scripture are criticized and rejected as unlearned men. If they find a Christian mistaken in a field in which they themselves know well and hear him maintaining his foolish opinions about our books, how are they going to believe those books in matters concerning the resurrection of the dead, the hope of eternal life, and the kingdom of heaven, when they think their pages are full of falsehoods on facts which they themselves have learnt from experience and the light of reason?[6]

That's a long quotation, but Augustine makes several crucial points. When it comes to the relationship of the creation story and evolutionary biology, we needn't get too worried about the apparent conflict. The book of Genesis was intended to answer different questions, questions like the ones we explored earlier. This is controversial stuff in some corners of contemporary Christianity, but as the North African bishop is dead, he's at no risk of receiving a horrific number of critical emails.

At the risk of receiving a horrific amount of email myself, I'd suggest that Augustine's words point us in the right direction for considering the question of the historicity of these early chapters of Genesis. There well may be some interesting parallels between scientific theories and the biblical story of origins. Any story we tell about how the cosmos came into being is called a **cosmogony**. Maybe some of the current scientific cosmogonies and the biblical one are different ways of describing the same series of events. That's why some theologians speak of the first eleven chapters of Genesis as a saga: something that isn't quite a historical, observer-based account but something that isn't disconnected from events in space and time either. Thinking that it must be one or the other is, for my old friend Karl Barth, a "ridiculous and middle-class habit of the modern Western mind," which suffers from a chronic lack of imagination.[7]

The point of the early chapters of Genesis is to tell us something important about why things are the way they are, why the world seems both beautiful and treacherous, why it's endlessly intriguing, and why taking on good tasks feels right. This is the sort of doctrine Genesis is meant to inform. These opening chapters help us see things in a certain way. They show us that the deep current of reality is grace, and that everything that isn't God—from glacial streams and open savannah to you and me—comes into being as a gift.

4

THEY WERE ASHAMED

Fallen Creatures

The world is wider in all directions, more dangerous and bitter, more extravagant and bright. We are making hay when we should be making whoopee; we are raising tomatoes when we should be raising Cain and Lazarus.
—Annie Dillard

One of Christianity's greatest modern critics, the very mustachioed Friedrich Nietzsche (1844–1900), argued that the Christian life was an attempt by the weak to rule the powerful. Weak religious people—pastors and professors, maybe even theology students and zealous congregants—use shame to get others to submit to an unnatural life. Religious leaders might use the threat of hell to make sure the strong can't lure all available sexual partners for themselves. They might talk about the moral risks of wealth to convince successful business folks to donate to the church. Through this sort of resentful conniving, religious people get in the way of human flourishing.

That's not what you thought your pastor was doing last Sunday, but it's what Nietzsche saw. With this in mind, we come to the second chapter of Genesis, which is something like a second creation story. Chapter 1 briefly told us about God's creation of the human creature; chapter 2 expands and retells the same story. Together they give us a picture of the character, value, and purpose of people. The chapters that follow expand this narrative description. As Nietzsche would surely point out, these are all contested ideas.

KEEPERS OF EARTH AND CULTURE

In light of God, what does it mean to be human? When we ask questions like this, questions about what it means to be a person, we enter territory known as **theological anthropology**. When we speak theologically about being human, we begin by noting that we are talking about creatures. A person is a part of creation and the product of a creative act. If you have ever camped in territory where large carnivores live, you know what part of this feels like. It feels like you're just another potential food source. Being a creature means each of us has more in common with spiders and zebras than with God. Talking this way might make some of us nervous. Maybe we've heard about the way some philosophers equate infants with pets. That isn't the intention. The point is to clarify that we aren't gods and aren't even crea*tors*, at least not in the same way God is.

We feel better, maybe, when we add the word *human* to the description. To be a person is to be a *human creature*. Humans are conscious of their presence in a place and in history in ways a grizzly bear is not. The Genesis story says that humans are the only creatures crafted in God's image. This is why, as we read in Genesis 9, we shouldn't kill each other. In the ancient world, emperors placed images of themselves in prominent spots throughout their territory. It was a sign of the emperor's territorial claim. We still do this today. You might have seen footage of American soldiers invading Iraq and pulling down images of Saddam Hussein. For human creatures to bear God's image is a sign that wherever they are, that place is God's. The unique status is amplified in the biblical story when God grants human creatures "dominion" (Genesis 1:26). That word is controversial today because some Christians have used it to excuse environmental destruction. However, Psalm 145 describes God's dominion with words like *gracious* and *merciful*. God is "good to all" and "upholds all who are falling." To be granted dominion in this case means to be given the responsibility of caring for something that is not ours.

To be a human creature is to be tasked. The unique character of this task is explained further in Genesis 2 with these words: "The LORD God took the man and put him in the garden of Eden to till it and keep it" (v. 15). And just a few verses later, "Whatever the man called every living creature, that was its name" (v. 19). The work of science and culture are right there: to care for the garden and to understand the earth's creatures. Some might be distracted by the reference to a *man*, but this is the stuff of *human* existence. I'm reminded of an Anglican prayer that thanks God for "tasks which demand our best efforts, and for leading us to accomplishments which satisfy and delight us." All it takes to know what this means is a day doing work that's challenging and engaging. Art and architecture, biology and the bassoon—all are part of God's good world.

FALLING UP AND FALLING DOWN

So far in this book we've mostly referred to words and speech in positive ways. However, the problems in Genesis start with words too—words about words, actually. The serpent asks Eve, "Did God say . . . ?" This is the beginning of a theological conversation. To be human is to speak and listen, to interpret and to learn whom to trust. It's obvious that the neatly ordered existence described earlier in Genesis doesn't fully depict the world we know. The story of creation may begin with rock-bottom claims about the goodness of the world and the special responsibility of human creatures, yet without something more it would seem too precious to be real.

In her beautifully written book *Pilgrim at Tinker Creek*, Annie Dillard develops a literary version of what we often call **natural theology**. Natural theology is a description of God and the world done with little reference to special revelation. She wrote the book while living in Virginia's Blue Ridge Mountains. I first read it when I was staying in a small rented apartment in the same part of the country. I had moved there to continue my theological education. I liked the history of the region and the way Virginia stretched from the Atlantic Ocean to the Appalachian Mountains. My little apartment was in the Shenandoah Valley. Dillard had lived farther south, on the other side of the Blue Ridge. She was taken with the natural beauty of that part of the world. She writes glowingly about the loveliness of trees when light shines through them just right, and about the playfulness of birds, who seem sometimes to do things for nothing more than the joy of it.

What makes Dillard's writing so profound is that she isn't romantic: she sees a shadow side to nature. One summer she was looking for frogs and noticed one that didn't jump away from her. It suddenly deflated—or at least that's how it looked. A giant water bug had latched on to the amphibian, injected it with a paralyzing enzyme, then shot it full of a toxin that dissolved its organs. Then, like a kid sucking down a milkshake, the bug had sucked everything out of the frog's skin.[1] The business of our world is conducted under death's shadow. If Scripture didn't acknowledge this, it would be hard for us to find it relevant. We refer to the beginning of this discussion in Genesis as the account of the **fall**. That's probably the heading that stands above Genesis 3 in your Bible.

Few of us need convincing that something isn't right in the world. We recognize that our sense of *ought* implies a difference between some ideal and the reality we experience. Few of us think that what we or our neighbors do is perfectly good. To say that Europeans shouldn't have forced Christianity on Indigenous peoples in other parts of the world assumes an *ought*—a morality—that is more than opinion. In the language of Christian theology, this discrepancy is described as fallenness. When we do what we ought not do, which is one of the implications of the fall, we sin.

Sin is a difficult word that travels with a lot of baggage. However, just about everyone believes in sin in one form or another. We might admit that some of our desires are ultimately harmful or that some of our actions or the actions of someone else violate our sense of what ought to happen. In the beginning of Genesis, this comes into the picture when Adam and Eve disregard God's directive. God's speech and the creation that flows from it leave space for just this sort of thing—for doubting the One most faithful. One explanation that Christians have given for the existence of pain and suffering is that a world with the freedom for sin seems on the whole to be better than a world in which humans are programmed for obedience. To get the goodness of freedom, sin comes along in the bargain.

Sin is the distortion of the relationship between Creator and creature, the innocence of trust replaced with the hubris of knowledge. Genesis says that the eyes of Adam and Eve were opened. The result is shame and fear. Because the distortion of this relationship is so fundamental, it becomes the distortion of all relationships. One of the best definitions for sin that I've come across is from a theologian named Cornelius Plantinga Jr.

Plantinga defines sin "as culpable shalom-breaking."[2] *Shalom* is a Hebrew word that means peace. Yet it doesn't refer to a peace that is merely the absence of conflict; it means peace and justice, the sort of peace that is connected to flourishing. Describing sin as "shalom-breaking" is important, because it reminds us that sin is a distortion of a very good thing. It means that God doesn't oppose sin for some arbitrary reason. God opposes it because it wrecks the goodness of things. God is opposed to sin because God is *for* shalom.

One point of tension within Christian circles is whether sin is best understood as personal and individual or as social and political. Peruvian theologian Gustavo Gutiérrez says that "sin is regarded as a social, historical fact, the absence of brotherhood and love in relationships among men, and, therefore, an interior, personal fracture."[3] Gutiérrez is regarded as the father of **liberation theology**, which is a contemporary theological approach that interprets the Bible with an emphasis on things related to the poor and oppressed. This is a valuable corrective to a theological tradition that has often been used to preserve the status quo. All theology is political, but liberation theology is more obviously so. For this reason, theologians like Gutiérrez are usually said to advocate a social and political view of sin. However, the quotation above suggests that the distinction might not be so clear.

I am not sure we have to choose. Shalom-breaking is pervasive enough that we should see it happening at both the individual level and the social level. Another crunchy theological term, **total depravity**, captures the scope of the problem. This is one of the ways we speak of how every part of our individual and collective selves is affected by sin: our desires, our thinking, our will, our use of power, our organizations—basically, everything. This doesn't mean any of us are worthless or as bad as we could be; it just means that nothing is unaffected by this thorough distortion of relationships. We are both victims and perpetrators of sin. Sin is both a condition we are in and something we do. It isn't the same as natural disasters or normal human limitation. The fact that most of us can't dunk a basketball is not the result of our sinful condition; the fact that our inability makes us jealous *is*.

Because of the shame of Adam and Eve, an animal, one of God's creatures, must be killed to provide them with a covering. Just as ice cracks when you step on a frozen puddle, so the lines of fracture quickly spread. Good relationships die, and so do animals and people. Before long, one of Adam and Eve's sons kills another. In Romans, Paul says that "sin came into the world through one man, and death came through sin" (Romans 5:12). Was there really no death before sin? The current scientific consensus is that a host of creatures lived and died long before humans walked the earth. It's probably better for us to think of the death brought about by sin as deeper than biology. The death that is connected to sin is a deep death, the death of relationship and community. Ultimately, it is the death of the most intimate of all relationships: the separation of creature from Creator.

MAKING A NAME FOR OURSELVES

The multistranded description of sin that emerges from Genesis is important for connecting the world we experience with the biblical narrative. Yet even more ultimately significant is God's response. In Genesis 3, God responds to the serpent's deception by saying, "I will put enmity between you and the woman, and between your offspring and hers; he will strike your head, and you will strike his heel" (v. 15). Notice that God's reaction points toward restoration. The phrase "he will strike your head" means that the serpent's power wouldn't go unchecked. We refer to this using the Latin term **protoevangelium**, which means "first gospel" or "prologue to the gospel." The woman's offspring would ultimately triumph over the powers of deception. God's grace and love are more significant than evil. This important foreshadowing, however, is only a passing break in the clouds. We see the clouds thickening and swirling in Genesis 6, which includes a bizarre story about the Nephilim. Whatever historical value the passage intends, the essential point about the world is simply that the wickedness of human creatures was "great in the earth" (v. 5). It results in God pressing a cataclysmic reset button: a flood, followed by a new beginning with the family of Noah.

The story of Noah essentially halves the primeval history of Genesis. The account of the flood, from the end of chapter 8 onward, functions literarily as a second creation story. If you read it closely, you'll notice several parallels to the early chapters of Genesis. One difference, though, is that Noah and his family are given animals as food. In Genesis 1, God only gave plants. In the story of Noah the grip of death is pretty tight. God specifically says that anyone who sheds the blood of another human will be called to give an account of their actions. Yet it is in this story that we find an expression of **common grace**: God promises Noah and every living creature to never be so destructive again.

God's engagement with Noah takes the form of a **covenant**. This is an important concept. A covenant was an ancient contract, the sort of thing usually drawn up between an overlord and a subservient people. Covenants contained these basic elements: a description of the two parties, the expectations of their relationship, and finally, the consequence for keeping or breaking the agreement. Covenants define a relationship. Near the end of Genesis 6, we hear God addressing Noah in this ancient form, "I will establish my covenant with you" (v. 18). This is the first time the word *covenant* shows up in Scripture, and it marks the beginning of a key biblical theme. Scholars commonly identify five formal covenants in the Bible. In addition to the one made with Noah, there's one made with Abraham, one with all Israel on Mount Sinai, one with David, and then there is the new covenant. Although each covenant has specific features, all of them point to the same general characteristic of the Creator: God is one who ties himself to creatures. This willingness itself is an important revelation of divine character.

After the flood, the story of the Tower of Babel initiates a key shift in the focus of the biblical story. The Babel story has two important features. The first is the people's goal to "make a name for ourselves" (Genesis 11:4). Here we see that sin can take the form of thinking too highly of oneself. This passage represents the temptation of human culture to usurp God and points to the second important feature of the story: sin can also take the form of rejecting diversity and rejecting God's directive to inhabit the earth's nooks and crannies in unique and place-dependent ways. The tower builders fear being "scattered abroad upon the face of the whole earth" (v. 4). God's response is to limit their idolatrous power by scrambling their words. God gives the gift of linguistic diversity.

The idolatrous capacity of human culture depicted in the Babel story does not blot out the more fundamental goodness of it. During the years I studied in Alberta and Virginia, I learned to appreciate the Indigenous heritage of the Great Plains and the small farms of the Shenandoah Valley. I walked hills and coulees that were special places for First Nations and met farm families who had stewarded land for generations. These kinds of cultural accompaniments of nature are fascinating and beautiful. The biblical story begins in a garden and ends in a city. This trajectory implies that the gift of history—the patience of God despite the fall—is for making something more of God's good creation. And yet the Babel story demonstrates that even though culture is good, specific cultures are never faultless.

The story of Babel sets up a vast parenthetical movement in God's restorative work. Within this important parenthesis are the lives of Abraham and Sarah and their descendants. On the other side is the story of Pentecost. On both sides of this parenthetical,

God deals with humanity in a universal way. As I noted in an earlier chapter, one of the central characteristics of the Christian faith is the assumption that the message is translatable. Kwame Bediako, a Ghanaian theologian, points out that just as early Christians learned to describe their faith in the thought forms of Greco-Roman culture, so Christians elsewhere must carry out the same work. For Bediako, becoming a Christian meant that he became *more* African, not less. He writes, "Christianity is no less Christian for being mediated through African languages, whilst Western Christianity does not enshrine universal standards."[4] Christians are those who tell the story of God's creative and restorative work in all corners of the world. Christians are those who recognize that the biblical story affirms certain aspects of our cultures and challenges others.

AUGUSTINE'S DREAMS AND YOU

Augustine, as you may recall, was from the same continent as Bediako, but he was an African of a much older vintage. In the fifth century, Augustine was involved in a historic exchange with a monk from Britain named Pelagius (354–420). At some point Pelagius traveled to Rome, where he was shocked at the immorality he found. Modern visitors to Rome aren't necessarily surprised by this, but Pelagius was. He was especially disturbed by the moral laxity of Christians. So he launched an investigation. He discovered that the locals believed moral purity was a gift from God, something that didn't require effort on their part. This was opposite to his own hardline asceticism. The attitude he found was congruent with Augustine's famous prayer, "Give what you command, and command what you will."[5] If God didn't give you the desire to stop stealing your neighbor's Wi-Fi, then God must not be commanding you to stop—or so the thinking went.

Those lines from Augustine come from his frustration with being unable to control his sexual desire. Earlier in life he had sensed God calling him to give up his mistress of more than a dozen years and to even forgo marriage. He was obedient in both cases, yet he still dreamed about sex and he still found himself wanting to have that part of his old life. His prayer, then, was a request to God for the ability to be obedient. What Pelagius saw, however, was people being let off the hook. He interpreted their behavior as not worrying about restraining themselves unless they felt like it.

After leaving town, Pelagius wrote a sort of indictment. He argued that humans can naturally live sinless lives and should do their best to do so: involuntary dreams about sex are no excuse for a lack of personal discipline. Augustine wasn't convinced, and the resulting controversy has defined the way many Christians understand sin and grace.

Pelagius believed our knowledge of right and wrong and our rationality are evidence of God's grace. If sin couldn't be avoided, he thought, God would be unjust to hold us accountable. His opponents, which in addition to Augustine included a monk named Jerome (345–420), charged him with denying **original sin**. Jerome lived in a cell in Bethlehem. He and Augustine said that Pelagius believed it was possible to live without sin and possible even to achieve salvation without grace.

A helpful way to think of original sin is to think of sin as unavoidable: because of the human condition, we all break shalom and can't avoid it. Original sin can refer to more than that, though. A key passage is one I mentioned earlier, Romans 5:12. Some, Augustine included, interpret this passage to mean that everyone automatically inherits Adam's guilt; his act was the "original sin" that implicates us all.[6] That's what some mean by the phrase. But many, if not most, modern biblical scholars would disagree with this way of reading Romans. They would suggest that while the passage clearly communicates the view that death and sin are unavoidable, Paul didn't necessarily mean that everyone is saddled with Adam's guilt. Yet even if Adam's sin doesn't make us guilty in some legal sense, there is still value in speaking of our universal complicity in betraying God's intention of shalom. This is no small thing when many of us profit from privilege and inequality by accident of our birth. Our solidarity as human creatures, what we might call our being "in Adam," means that we share in the burden of sin.

You've probably guessed that contemporary scientific understandings of human origins might play a role in this conversation as well. Does our understanding of sin require the actual historical existence of Adam and Eve? If we are willing to think of the account of the fall, whether historical or not, as speaking to the realities of the situation we find ourselves in, the challenge is not serious. The way the Bible describes the sinful choice of Eve and Adam, along with the resulting relational disfigurement and the reign of hyper-death, surely describes our collective situation well. If you've ever had a friend who wants to make some positive changes in her life but can't because of the negative influence of her family, you have a sense of this. We are all in this together, but because of sin, we are too often alone.

5

From the LAND of UR

Mission

A beginning is that which is not itself necessarily after anything else, and which has naturally something else after it; an end is that which is naturally after something itself, either as its necessary or usual consequent, and with nothing else after it; and a middle, that which is by nature after one thing and has also another after it. A well-constructed plot, therefore, cannot either begin or end at any point one likes.
—Aristotle

At the end of the eleventh chapter of Genesis we stumble across a turn in Scripture that contradicts one of the central assumptions of our own time. The passage tells the story of Noah's descendants; however, we quickly notice that it doesn't tell us about all of them. The writer's attention is drawn to just one couple—Abram and Sarai. The family tree works its way down, branch to branch, to these two. In Genesis 11:31 we are pulled into the prelude of a new scene: "Terah took his son Abram and his grandson Lot son of Haran, and his daughter-in-law Sarai, his son Abram's wife, and they went out together from Ur of the Chaldeans to go into the land of Canaan; but when they came to Haran, they settled there." Abram's brother was already dead, and soon Terah would be as well.

Most of us have been taught to value universality and fairness. We want access to our bank accounts from anywhere. We want the same laws to apply equally to everyone. In an age like ours, the tightening of focus to this one family is strange, almost scandalous.

OUR FATHER ABRAHAM

When I finished my studies in Alberta, I knew I was just scratching the surface. I wanted to think more seriously about the relationship of the Christian faith to the forces of consumerism and nationalism. I wanted to learn more about the history of the Scriptures. I also wanted to be closer to home. So, as I mentioned earlier, I enrolled in a graduate program at a school in Virginia. It was only a few hours' drive from where I went to elementary and high school. Reading the story of Abram's calling can feel a little like going back to visit a school you attended when you were young. A place that once contained almost everything that mattered suddenly seems small and unimportant.

Amid the swirl of various faith traditions and other forms of spirituality, it can feel a little silly to take Christian claims seriously. Sometimes we might feel a bit naïve for "believing all that stuff" or for doubting that everyone's perspective can be "true for them." Some theologians, most notably a Brit named John Hick, have made alternative suggestions. Hick became an evangelical Christian in university, but later in life he adopted a more pluralist perspective. Hick came to believe that since we can't know transcendent reality directly, all we have are our own perceptions of it. Different religions, he concluded, are rooted in different cultural expressions of these varied perceptions. This form of **pluralism** is attractive in several senses. However, it ultimately assumes that someone is in a position to say authoritatively that each faith does have some truth in it. It's hard to see who could stand above these competing truth claims and make such a determination. To paraphrase one Mennonite theologian: every adolescent's breath of fresh air is someone else's intellectual ghetto. What seems like an objective perspective on the beliefs of others is always just one more view from one more place.

I like how the mystical theologian Julian of Norwich (1342–1416) turns things inside out. Julian is famous for her visions of Jesus. She describes one of them like this:

> And in this vision he showed me a little thing, the size of a hazel-nut, lying in the palm of my hand, and to my mind's eye it was as round as any ball. I looked at it and thought, "What can this be?" And the answer came to me, "It is all that is made." I wondered how it could last, for it was so small I thought it might suddenly disappear. And the answer in my mind was, "It lasts and will last for ever because God loves it; and in the same way everything exists through the love of God." In this little thing I saw three attributes: the first is that God made it, the second is that he loves it, the third is that God cares for it.[1]

It's quite possible that Julian wasn't actually the name of the woman who had this vision. The name might just be a reference to the church where she was holed up. We do know that this part of her vision says something powerful about the scope of our world in relationship to God. It reminds us that God is content to work through small things—through frail, fragile, fractious things. The Creator works through channels within creation rather than overwhelming it from the outside. The calling of Abram and Sarai is a small thing in creation, not a tsunami. That this would be the way of God surprises us because it is not how power usually looks.

In the first verse of Genesis 12 we read that God spoke to Abram, saying, "Go from your country and your kindred and your father's house to the land that I will show you." God promised to make a "great nation" of Abram and his wife, but not because Abram had somehow managed to manipulate God, to press the right buttons, or to offer the right sacrifices. God promised this in order to do something for the world at large. "I will bless you," God says in the next verse, "so that you will be a blessing . . . and in you all the families of the earth shall be blessed."

The covenant between God and Abram is formalized later in Genesis 15–17. It is significant that Abram's name is changed to Abraham and Sarai's to Sarah. The core of the covenant is that Abraham would need to walk before God in obedience. God would provide the land and offspring required to make this visible to the world. The agreement would be marked in the flesh of every male descendant with the significant and unmistakable sign of circumcision. What follows the creation of this covenant is a drama presented to the rest of the world. In the subsequent acts the identity of the Creator will become increasingly clear. So too will the distance between the way of things as we know it and the Creator's intent. It will be in the context of this drama that God will begin to repair the ruptures in shalom.

THE NARROWNESS OF ELECTION AND THE BREADTH OF DIVINE LOVE

As I moved deeper into my theological studies, one of the terms I ran into time and again was **election**. I learned that the word is pretty important for how some Christians talk about this narrowing of focus in the early part of the Bible. Theologians sometimes refer to this narrowing as the "scandal of particularity." I shared that phrase with a group of parishioners once. They laughed at it. It's a bit too dramatic. But still, the idea that God would work to address universal problems through one family (or even one nation or one faith tradition) makes us squirm in our seats. *Election*, in theological conversation, has nothing to do with democracy and everything to do with God choosing some to bless all.

In his letter to the Romans, Paul wrestles with the idea of election. In Romans 9:19-24, he reminds readers that the precise workings of God's choices can only be known by God. Alluding to the great philosophical book of Job, Paul writes, "Will what is molded say to the one who molds it, 'Why have you made me like this?'" (Romans 9:20). This is one of the strongest descriptions of God's freedom and creaturely inferiority in all of Scripture. To paraphrase Paul, what if God molded some containers just to be destroyed? What is that to us? If God is the one who holds all that is, what right do we have to think such a being owes us an explanation? As I plunged deeper into the history of theology, I learned that the tension many of us see between God's broad love and the decision to work through a few was not lost on early theologians.

Late in the fourth century, the bishop of Nyssa was a remarkable man named Gregory (335–94). Nyssa was in what would now be the Central Anatolia region of Turkey—just in case you happen to know your Turkish regions. Gregory was a part of a group of theologians we often refer to as the Cappadocians. They came from a region by that name. In addition to Gregory of Nyssa, the group included his older brother, known as Basil of Caesarea (329–79); their oldest sister and spiritual mentor, Macrina (330–79); and a close friend named Gregory of Nazianzus (329–90).

The Cappadocians have been and still are especially influential in the Orthodox tradition. It's worth knowing that the Western, or "Catholic," segment of Christianity and the capital O Orthodox tradition formally parted ways in 1054. That's about five hundred years before the Protestant Reformation. However, on an informal level, the two communities had been in separate worlds long before that. They disagreed over the power of the bishop of Rome, who became known as the pope, and how best to describe the relationship of the Holy Spirit and Jesus. Catholics and the Orthodox agreed that it made sense to say that the Son and the Spirit "proceed" from the Father. However, they disagreed on whether it's wise to say that the Spirit also proceeds from the Son. It's a fairly technical point of trinitarian doctrine known as the *filioque* controversy. Perhaps more practically, the two traditions tended toward separate ways because the Catholics spoke Latin, while the Orthodox spoke Greek.

One of the things that stand out about the early Orthodox theologian Gregory of Nyssa is that he was one of the first Christian theologians to adamantly oppose slavery. He writes, "If God does not enslave what is free, who is he that sets his own power above God's?"[2] Gregory also made significant contributions to the way Christians understand the triune character of God. More germane to our discussion of God's covenant with Abraham, Gregory was something of a universalist. **Universalism** is the belief that God's love means that everyone will ultimately be redeemed. In a treatise called *On the Soul and Resurrection*, Gregory writes:

> It is plain . . . from the Holy Scripture that God becomes, to those who deserve it, locality, and home, and clothing, and food, and drink, and light, and riches, and dominion, and everything thinkable, and nameable that goes to make our life happy. But He that becomes "all" things will be "in all" things too; and herein it appears to me that Scripture teaches the complete annihilation of evil. If, that is, God will be "in all" existing things, evil; plainly, will not then be amongst them; for if any one was to assume that it did exist then, how will the belief that God will be "in all" be kept intact?[3]

Gregory is reflecting on another passage from Paul's writings, this one from 1 Corinthians 15. Gregory follows Paul in believing that when we die, the divine Creator and Judge will cleanse us from evil. Then, since we're purified, we will be united with the source of all goodness. Notice that Gregory's universalism is quite different from John Hick's pluralism. Gregory doesn't rely on a distinction between how we perceive God and how God really is. Instead, his view is built on the inclusiveness of God's loving power.

Gregory explains his position through the voice of his sister Macrina. He refers to her as "the Teacher." Macrina was dying when Gregory wrote the piece to which I'm referring. Some scholars think Gregory's universalism is hard to square with his strong affirmation of human freedom. If we are free, aren't we free to reject God? In any event, Gregory's comments represent one way of describing the missionary embrace of God. If God is "all in all," if "all things are subjected to him" (1 Corinthians 15:28), why would God's restorative love not overwhelm our desire to have things our way? To place this in the context of the story of Abraham, maybe Abraham's role isn't as exclusive as it first seems. Maybe it signals God's intention to redeem every creature tasked to keep and to work the earth. The question has been debated by thoughtful Christians since at least the time of Origen (185–254). Origen predated Gregory by about a century, but he too is known for supporting universal salvation.

We should discuss a third common approach. In addition to universalism, the idea that God saves everyone through Christ, and pluralism, the idea that all religions are equally valid, there is another view, one that usually bears the label **exclusivism**. Advocates of this widely held perspective sometimes prefer the term **particularism**. Regardless of the label, this view highlights the limited and discretionary character of God's saving work. In this perspective, restoration is limited to those who actively and intentionally respond to God's redeeming work in Christ. The contemporary tone of the debate between the universalist and the exclusivist positions is captured well in the titles of books written by two dapper American pastors: Rob Bell's *Love Wins* and Francis Chan's critical response, *Erasing Hell*. Of course, as we'll see later, one doesn't have to erase hell or deny that love wins to find other perspectives that do justice to Scripture.

Questions like this can sound pretty theoretical, especially when we realize that we can't empirically validate one view or another. Yet in another sense this isn't theoretical at all. Some of the most serious conversations any of us will ever have are connected to death and whatever comes after it. For Christians, the difference between universalism and exclusivism is significant, but not usually so much so that those on one side believe those on the other aren't still members of the faith. The same recognition isn't always granted to pluralists, who see members of all faith traditions as blindfolded folks touching different parts of the same animal. One of the things that hold Christians' perspectives about these matters together is the shared understanding that, however it works precisely, God is ultimately the one in charge. This conviction comes from the account of creation we discussed a few chapters ago, especially the truth that God brings order out of chaos. God does not have to negotiate with some other authority or strike a deal with some ultra-god or sub-god. The calling of Abraham and Sarah is an extension of this. God elects and summons . . . the ancient nomads respond.

A MISSION OF BLESSING

God's covenant with Abraham and his family is certainly a blessing, but it's a blessing with a purpose. The covenant is also an act of self-disclosure on God's part. It shows that the Creator is not only transcendent and unknowable but also willing to be bound to a particular family for the purpose of blessing the world.

God nurtures a distinct family, a distinct tribe, and eventually a distinct nation to serve as a display model or demonstration plot. When you drive through farming country in a place like Virginia's Shenandoah Valley, you sometimes see signs beside a field indicating that it's been planted with some new type of seed. The signs are to show other farmers what's possible. That's what God intended to do with the descendants of Sarah and Abraham, including ancient Israel and, eventually, the church.

The global theological conversation has returned repeatedly to the implications of how God will bless the many through the few. For instance, in 1974 some 2,300 Christian leaders from 150 countries gathered in Lausanne, Switzerland. Loosely defined as a gathering of evangelicals, this group included well-known teachers such as Francis Schaeffer, John Stott, and the preacher who got things going—Billy Graham. *Time* magazine said the Lausanne Congress, as it became known, may have been the most diverse meeting of Christians ever. The meeting was about Christian outreach.

One of the most striking achievements of the gathering was the production of a "covenant" to proclaim "God's good news for the whole world" and to "make disciples of every nation."[4] Calling it a covenant was obviously a nod to the biblical arrangements we've described. Thousands of people signed the Lausanne Covenant. However, differences arose over whether something should be said about the social implications of the Christian message. One group, sometimes referred to as the "radical evangelicals," believed that being followers of Jesus and sharing his message demanded a response to poverty and a critique of the social and economic injustice at its root.

Among this group, and a key player in the congress as a whole, was a Peruvian theologian and activist named Samuel Escobar. Escobar gave a talk in which he referred to the way Jesus defined his ministry: "To preach the Gospel to the poor; / To heal the brokenhearted, / To preach deliverance to the captives / and recovering of sight to the blind, / To set at liberty them that are bruised." Jesus was quoting Isaiah. Escobar concluded his paper by noting the challenges to such an all-encompassing agenda: "We live in a fallen world which is trapped in injustice and sin, and what happens at the political and financial level is what also happens in our own personal daily life."[5] His words align well with our discussion of sin in the previous chapter.

Although their perspective was not unopposed, Escobar and his group were largely successful in getting the larger group to agree that missionary witness had to address poverty and other social issues. The fifth article of the Lausanne Covenant affirmed that Christians should share Jesus' concern "for justice and reconciliation throughout human society and for the liberation of men and women from every kind of oppression. Because men and women are made in the image of God, every person, regardless of race, religion, colour, culture, class, sex or age, has an intrinsic dignity because of which he or she should be respected and served, not exploited." The ninth article was more specific, saying, "All of us are shocked by the poverty of millions and disturbed by the injustices which cause it. Those of us who live in affluent circumstances accept our duty to develop a simple life-style in order to contribute more generously to both relief and evangelism."[6]

It seems to me that the holistic view of the gospel and Christian mission taken by these evangelical radicals aligns with the biblical vision. In 2012, this basic conviction—that the Christian faith is necessarily practical and concerned with contemporary challenges—was upheld by a follow-up consultation addressing the importance of caring for God's creation. That sounds like a recovery of the basic human task from Genesis of caring for the earth.

This all sounds good. However, the actual history of the way Christians have inherited the mission of Abraham and Sarah is not so pure. Four years after the Lausanne Congress, Samuel

Escobar cowrote a little book called *Christian Mission and Social Justice*. Near the beginning of the book, Escobar relates part of the plot from a novel, *La casa verde* (*The Green House*), by Peruvian novelist Mario Vargas Llosa. The Green House in the book's title is a brothel on Peru's northern coast. One of the characters is a young girl, brought from the Amazon jungle by missionaries. The missionaries try to "civilize" and Christianize the young woman. Shorn of her family and culture, she ends up working in the Green House. Escobar points out that Vargas Llosa did his homework in writing the novel; this sort of thing actually happened.[7]

The church has conspired with governments and industry in deeply destructive ways. Canadian churches, for example, are still learning about the devastating effects on Indigenous people of our collusion with colonialist agendas. In this country that meant the creation of residential schools designed to, among other things, assimilate Indigenous persons and destroy their cultural legacy. These sorts of things are a part of our history, and there's no getting around it. What this means is that Christians cannot read the Bible or talk about the mission of God without recognizing our damnable past. Escobar believes that a key aspect of an appropriate Christian sense of mission should be the conviction that faith does not align with any specific political system. The people of God are unique, and are not identifiable with any nation or bluntly connected to any political ideology. When we forget that, we tend to use God rather than serve God.

In a similar way, the early church did not see its mission as furthering the goals of the Roman Empire. They knew that no nation and no community of faith is beyond critique. One of the things we'll observe as we follow the story of Abraham and Sarah's children is that they are subject to divine correction. The God of Abraham is the one the psalmist refers to when he writes, "The LORD looks down from heaven; he sees all humankind. From where he sits enthroned he watches all the inhabitants of the earth" (Psalm 33:13-14). Abraham and Sarah are blessed so that through them God would bless the world. Yet it is in this family that we see the beginnings of a community whose very life is to signify the presence and call of God. They are to demonstrate to the world the divine prescription for justice and flourishing.

6

LET THEM GO
and GATHER STRAW
for THEMSELVES

Slavery

I've always lived here, so did my father and grandfather. We've always been here and we've always worked for the same master. When my father died I had to take over his debt; that was almost thirty years ago.
  —**Shivraj, in *Disposable People* by Kevin Bales**

The God who creates is also the God who sets us free. That's what the biblical story reveals. What we need to recognize, though, is that slavery is not a thing of the past. Sociologist Kevin Bales makes the startling claim that at the beginning of the twenty-first century, more people were enslaved than were "stolen from

Africa in the time of the transatlantic slave trade." A slave, he says, is someone who is totally controlled by someone else for the purpose of "economic exploitation."[1] What's almost as troubling as the scale is the fact that it isn't just the stereotypical organized crime boss making a profit—it's also those of us who own mutual funds and those of us who worry more about getting low-priced stuff than about the well-being of the people who make it. Active slavery at various points in the global supply chain lets us buy things cheaply and get good returns on our investments.

Modern slavery thrives because lives in many countries are cheap and because many traditional forms of support have been obliterated by the global economy. So many poor bodies are for sale. In some parts of our world, a brothel owner can make an 800 percent profit from the enslavement of a girl between the ages of twelve and fifteen—each year.[2]

A GOD OF FREEDOM

Slavery is a real, physical experience for far too many people. Even as we begin to think of slavery and freedom in more general terms, we should not forget this. But this most abhorrent and extreme form of slavery is a part of a broader aspect of the common human experience. We all find ourselves, with seeming inevitability, doing things that keep ourselves and others in bondage.

If you've ever seen an image of Earth taken from space at night, you have a sense of the scale of what we're talking about. The city lights in these images show how people are clumping into ever-larger cities. In these images the East Coast of the United States is almost one long, bright slash. So is Japan and the eastern part of China. These urban centers are so full of human stories that it's hard to fathom.

Once, in the middle of one of those huge blotches of light, I met a man in his forties whose job was to lead privileged high school students on tours of the seamier side of the large city. The

urban guide showed them where sex workers picked up clients
and where people who were homeless slept. His own story paral-
leled the biographies of some of the young people he introduced
the students to on the streets. He grew up in an abusive family in
a small town. He left home as a teenager and migrated to the city,
where he survived by working as a prostitute and self-medicating
with drugs. His story is both singular and symbolic. Addictions,
cycles of domestic violence, generational trauma, consumerism,
and the desire for power: these are part of the human condition.
As a result, many of us are prodded in destructive directions. This
is surely why the themes of oppression and freedom surface again
and again in the biblical drama.

Many people have found encouragement in the fact that the
God who created also sets people free. Gustavo Gutiérrez, whom
we first met a couple of chapters ago, has pointed out that God's
being as Creator and as the one who freed Israel from slavery
are tied together throughout Scripture.[3] Think about Isaiah 43,
where the first verse reads: "But now thus says the LORD, he
who created you, O Jacob, he who formed you, O Israel: Do
not fear, for I have redeemed you; I have called you by name,
you are mine." The word *redeem* here means that God has paid
Israel's debt and bought back their freedom; we often speak of
God's work in Jesus as **redemption**. This is a word that comes
up regularly in theological conversation. What we see in Scripture
is that this characteristic of God, revealed so clearly in Jesus, is
an extension of the way God dealt with Israel. In fact, we can't
understand Jesus without understanding Israel's experience.

Think about the beginning of Jesus' life. In the gospel of Matthew an angel tells Joseph to take his little family and leave the
country. Herod wants to kill any competitors to his throne. So,
disguised by the darkness of night, Mary and Joseph take their
child and leave Bethlehem. They become refugees. Matthew says
that this journey to North Africa was intended to "fulfill what

had been spoken by the LORD through the prophet, 'Out of Egypt I have called my son'" (Matthew 2:15). The prophet in this case is Hosea. Here's the fascinating thing: In their original formulation, Hosea's words aren't related to Jesus. The relevant line in Hosea reads: "When Israel was a child, I loved him, and out of Egypt I called my son" (Hosea 11:1).

We'll get to the specifics of Israel's experience in a moment, but for now, notice how Matthew fudges things. He blurs the lines between a person and a nation. In doing so, he implies that the identity and the mandate of Israel and Jesus run together. The story lines parallel each other. God protects Israel/Jesus by taking them/him to Egypt. However, neither the mission of Israel nor that of Jesus could be fulfilled there, so both are brought back and set to work in the home country. So the story of Israel's enslavement in Egypt refers to a historical event in the lives of Abraham's descendants *and* to the life of Jesus. But that isn't all. For millennia, biblical readers have recognized that the story also symbolizes the way we are all bound by forces beyond our control. They've recognized too that the end of Israel's enslavement gives us hope for our own release from enslavement to the forces of sin and death.

In this way, a single Old Testament passage operates on several levels. Theologians in the Middle Ages called these layers of meaning the **quadriga**. The term literally referred to a chariot pulled by four horses. In theological conversation, though, it came to refer to the four levels on which we might read a passage from the Old Testament. On the **literal** level the reference to bondage in Egypt simply refers to the historical events involving Joseph and company. On the **eschatological** level it refers to our being stuck in a fallen world awaiting the freedom of the age to come. On the **typological** level it refers to Jesus' own refugee experience. And finally, on a **moral** level the story speaks to our being enslaved by sin and evil.

AND INTO EGYPT

Let's turn back and examine the original story. As you probably remember, God had promised Abraham and Sarah many descendants. God had Abraham look at the stars just to be sure he got the idea. The downside, as we read in Genesis 15, was that their offspring would be "aliens in a land that is not theirs." In the story of Joseph we learn how this happened.

Abraham's great-grandchildren made a living herding animals. They were the children of Jacob, a man who eventually became known as Israel. It so happened that a famine threatened to wipe the family out. Luckily, one of the brood, Joseph, had already made it big in Egypt. Pharaoh called him Zaphenath-paneah, gave him a serious gold necklace and a wife named Asenath. In Genesis 41 we read how Pharaoh decreed that without Joseph's approval, nobody in Egypt could "lift up hand or foot." When Israel's other children came to Egypt in search of food, Joseph was in a good position to help. Pharaoh gave them land and responsibility for his livestock in addition to their own. Traditional Egyptians were unimpressed with herders, but it appears that God used their prejudice to keep Israel's children from being absorbed into the broader Egyptian culture. The book of Genesis ends with the death of Jacob/Israel and shortly after that the death of Joseph himself. Joseph was a prototype of Christ (think of the typological reading I mentioned above). Joseph suffered personally but became Israel's savior and the savior of surrounding peoples.

Early in the first chapter of Exodus, we read that "the Israelites were fruitful and prolific; they multiplied and grew exceedingly strong, so that the land was filled with them" (v. 7). However, when a new Egyptian ruler came into power and the memory of Joseph faded, the Egyptian elite became worried about the number and power of these cattle herders. They demoted the Israelites to slaves. We discussed earlier that all people are created in the image of God; they aren't meant to be enslaved. What's more, Israel's children couldn't fulfill their mission of blessing the world when they lost their freedom. The book of Exodus, then, charts the way God frees them. And not just how God frees them *from* something but how God frees them *for* something: for being the sort of people through whom God could bless others.

SPEAKING ABOUT GOD

We have now begun to open up our description of God a little. Theology, as we said earlier, is mostly about God. Many other things come up in theological conversations, but our main subject is still God. As we've moved beyond describing God as transcendent and immanent and beyond speaking of God as the Creator, though, we have started using descriptions that could also be used for a person. When we say that God is "the redeemer" or "the savior" or "the liberator," we do so knowing that there are people who fit this description as well. The question that arises is how these terms can relate both to God and to creatures. This becomes challenging when we remember that God is entirely distinct from creation. Human creatures, even the really good ones like the chatty barista at your local coffee shop, have more in common with a rock than with God. If all that is true, how do these words we use to describe God say anything valuable at all?

We unfolded part of the answer earlier when we discussed divine revelation—the act of God's self-disclosure. We can speak of God as "redeemer" because God shares that with us. Creation serves as a sort of artistic medium—or to shift metaphors a bit, as a stage for God's self-revelation. God's act of creation is an act not only of forceful, wild development but also of tender, humble self-display. Throughout Scripture, then, God's self-revelation makes use of various cultural forms. In the book of Hosea, for instance, God is the rejected lover. In other parts of Scripture, God is a covenant maker, a warrior, a laboring woman.

Yet to say that God uses human institutions this way only deals with half the issue. It doesn't fully explain how the words of creatures can say anything worthwhile about their mysterious and holy Creator. How does human language have any relationship to God? This can get technical, but we can think about it a few different ways. First, it might be the case that the words we say about God could mean one thing when we use them to refer to God and another when we use them to speak about creaturely things. If this is the case, we would say that the language works **equivocally**. Alternatively, we could say that the words mean exactly the same thing in both cases. When we say that God is our savior, we mean that in exactly the same way it would be true of a helpful police officer. If this is the case we would say the language works **univocally**. Notice that neither option seems particularly helpful. In the first case, where language functions equivocally, saying that God is our savior has no relationship to what it might mean for a creature to be a savior. If that were true, we couldn't be sure what we meant when we spoke about God. Our theological speech would be no better than silence. Or maybe it would be *worse* than silence, because it would mislead us into thinking that we knew things about God when we really didn't. In the second case, where language functions univocally, we are forced to ignore the basic presupposition that God is transcendent and distinct from creation. That is troubling too.

You've probably guessed where this is going. When someone sets up an impossible choice, they usually want to either present a third option or sell you something (or both!). You could choose between the burger and the fries—*or* you could buy the full meal at a discount. In this case, it's Thomas Aquinas who gives us the third option. He suggests that our speech about God works **analogically**. Analogies are helpful because they use something we know to help us understand something we do not. There is never 100 percent correlation between the two objects in an analogy. If you compare your love to a rose, red or any other color, there are clearly similarities and differences. Your love is probably not the product of photosynthesis.

When we say that God is a redeemer, we don't mean that God must literally provide the devil with financial reimbursement. When we say that God is a savior or a warrior, neither term necessarily says the same things about the use of violence with respect to God as they would in the context of a human agent. This is even the case when we describe God as a father. To speak of God the Father is not to speak of a being with male genitalia and a beard or whatever. Some ancient theologians described God using the analogy of the sun. They didn't think God was exactly like the sun; rather, they thought our experience of this celestial object was similar in some ways to our experience of God. We speak about God using analogies.

A GOD OF DISRUPTION

The ambiguity of the words we use to describe God is one of the reasons it's important to speak of God's actions. In the book of Exodus, we see that God overturns the existing social order. Israel's children were enslaved; then God freed them. Just because they existed in one state didn't mean things would stay that way. In the parts of theological discussions that deal with morality, we generalize this observation and say that an *is* doesn't equal an *ought*.

One common misconception about theology is that it's mostly about abstract beliefs. For one reason or another, there is a tendency to separate beliefs about who God is from the way we live. Menno Simons (1496–1561), another sixteenth-century reformer and a one-time Catholic priest, wrote that "true knowledge begets love, and love begets obedience to the commandments of God." He continued in what has become a famous quotation:

> For true evangelical faith is of such a nature that it cannot lie dormant, but manifests itself in all righteousness and works of

love; . . . it destroys all forbidden lusts and desires; it seeks and
serves and fears God; it clothes the naked; it feeds the hungry;
it comforts the sorrowful; it shelters the destitute; it aids and
consoles the sad; . . . it serves those that harm it.[4]

For Menno, there's no such thing as faith or belief without
action. We might put it this way: you don't know the God of the
Bible if you aren't clothing and feeding those who don't have
what they need. Theology is a practical thing.

One of the great themes running throughout the Bible is God's
concern for those who are oppressed by the machinery of society.
So when we ask, "Who is God?" we might say that God is the one
who shows up in gracious, disruptive action on behalf of those
who suffer. This theme surfaces in God's liberation of Israel and,
as we'll see shortly, in the way of life God gives those freed slaves.
It is also a prominent theme in the Prophets and certainly in the
ministry of Jesus.

Sometimes preachers talk about the "heart of God." This is of
course another analogy. God doesn't have a literal heart. What
preachers mean is that certain things seem to take us right to the
core of who God is. One of the places where the Bible reveals
God's heart is in the very story we are discussing: the liberation of
the enslaved Israelites. Early in Exodus 6, God speaks to Moses in
a most striking and intimate way: "I appeared to Abraham, Isaac,
and Jacob as God Almighty, but by my name 'The LORD' I did not
make myself known to them" (v. 3). Several verses later Moses
hears God say, "I am the LORD, and I will free you from the burdens of the Egyptians and deliver you from slavery to them. . . . I
will take you as my people, and I will be your God" (vv. 6-7). God
reveals himself to Moses in a new way. The title LORD in English
Bibles is a substitution for God's covenant name, YHWH. When
Israel experiences God's freeing acts, they encounter the heart of
God. Who is God? God is the one who sets captives free and who
brings justice to the oppressed.

Not every story of liberation is quick and decisive. Personal liberation from destructive habits, relationships, or addictions is often slow, and progress is incremental. The story of Israel's liberation, by contrast, is dramatic. It involves walking sticks becoming snakes, a series of plagues, a false start, and finally an angel of death. A key part of the way the Bible narrates the story is the way it shows the LORD's power over the gods of the empire. It's written to make it abundantly clear that God is the one at work. This isn't always so clear in other accounts of liberation. Sometimes it seems unclear that we should credit God with anything at all. Sometimes we wonder if we can't fully explain things through psychology or politics or the laws of nature.

If we take a closer look at the drama of Exodus, we see that here too it can be hard to say exactly who or what is truly responsible. At the center of the story is the fickleness of the pharaoh. At one moment he seems ready to permit the Israelites to leave, the next he holds them fast. The biblical narration of the events seems as mercurial as Pharaoh himself. In some instances the writer seems to tell us that Pharaoh is responsible for his decision (e.g., Exodus 8:15; 9:34). In others we are given the impression that Pharaoh is only a tool and that his decisions are mandated by God (e.g., Exodus 4:21; 7:3; 9:12; 10:1). It is entirely possible that this shows the discordant roots of the text. By that I mean that these differing explanations may be because of differing ways the story was told before it was consolidated into the version we read today. However, the Christian tradition has also seen the story as a key example of something referred to as **concursus**. This term comes from Latin and refers to two things—two streams, maybe—running together. To say that Pharaoh is making up his mind doesn't mean we have to say God is not involved: the outcome can be the concursus of Pharaoh's action and God's. The point is that God carries out God's purposes through secondary means. A historian, working according to the professional standards of her discipline, would not be inclined to credit God with the liberation of Israel. Yet this is almost always the way God works in the world. There is always a material or historical explanation. When we say that God is a God of freedom, the implication is that God's Spirit is at work in the glimpses of liberation we see all around us.

LIBERATION

Since liberation plays such a prominent role in Scripture, it shouldn't be a surprise that many voices speak these themes into contemporary theology. As I mentioned earlier, the man known as the father of liberation theology is a Catholic priest from Peru named Gustavo Gutiérrez. He is famous for suggesting that God exercises a "preferential option for the poor." This means that God defends the dignity and the well-being of the poor. Gutiérrez's most famous book, *Teología de la liberación*, was originally published in 1971 and translated into English in 1973 as *A Theology of Liberation*. It begins this way:

> This book is an attempt at reflection, based on the Gospel and the experiences of men and women committed to the process of liberation in the oppressed and exploited land of Latin America. It is a theological reflection born of the experience of shared efforts to abolish the current unjust situation and to build a different society, freer and more human.[5]

For Gutiérrez, Christ's work can be characterized as liberation, or as the transition "from sin to grace, from slavery to freedom."[6] It is a gift of true communion with God and other people. It is important to notice that this isn't merely a spiritual experience. Liberation indicates the hopes and goals of oppressed peoples for freedom and self-determination. Liberation theology is one of the most significant developments in the theological conversation of the latter part of the twentieth century. Gutiérrez and other liberation theologians like Leonardo Boff, Jon Sobrino, and Juan Luis Segundo help Christians read Scripture, especially the epic of Exodus, with a seriousness that many overly privileged people would otherwise miss.

One of the things liberation theology highlights is the importance of context. Everyone's reading of the Bible is shaped, in varying degrees, by their social context. Thus Gutiérrez's work is directly tied to his Latin American context and the disparity in terms of wealth and political power between the rich and the poor. Many other theologians have developed similar points of emphasis. Black theology, for instance, emerged most notably from the experience of African Americans and now is an important point of reference for Black Christians around the world. Feminist theology grew from the experience of women in a faith that has often privileged men. Palestinian liberation theologians read the Bible in ways that highlight the problems associated with Zionism.

Many important voices are often associated with Gutiérrez. We will meet more later, but for now I want to introduce one more, a scholar named James Cone. Just as Gutiérrez is considered the father of Latin American liberation theology, so Cone carries similar importance for Black theology. Cone was born in the United States, in Arkansas to be more precise. As a child he experienced the racism of white Christians. So as an emerging scholar, he questioned the relevance of theology done by people with social privilege. He was especially struck by Malcolm X's claim that Christianity was a white man's religion. Cone became a professor of theology, and in 1970 published *A Black Theology of Liberation*. That was the same year he began teaching at Union Theological Seminary in New York City. Here are the book's opening lines: "The reader is entitled to know what to expect in this book. It is my contention that Christianity is essentially a religion of liberation. . . . Any message that is not related to the liberation of the poor in the society is not Christ's message. Any theology that is indifferent to the theme of liberation is not

Christian theology."[7] Cone goes on to say that in a society where the oppressed are Black, Christian theology must be identified with the goals of that community.

I wonder if you've ever introduced a friend to someone else by recounting a story: "This is the woman who walked the Camino de Santiago," or "This is the friend I told you about who raises sheep." Sometimes there are stories that virtually encapsulate a person. These stories are more helpful in describing someone than even sharing the person's given name. In the drama of the Bible, God's freeing of Israel from slavery isn't just one story among many. It is the foundational narrative that defines this people. It's even more than that; it is also the story that serves to define Israel's divine covenant partner. There is no more crucial example of this than in Exodus 6, where God says to Moses: "I will take you as my people, and I will be your God. You shall know that I am the LORD your God, who has freed you from the burdens of the Egyptians" (v. 7). That is who God is: the one who frees.

7

And **THEY WENT** *into the* **WILDERNESS**

Formation

When we see the world as an end in itself, everything becomes itself a value and consequently loses all value . . . . Things treated merely as things in themselves destroy themselves because only in God have they any life.
—**Alexander Schmemann**

One of the purest deposits of iron ore in the world lies on the north side of Baffin Island. This is remote country—not end-of-the-subway-line remote but above-the-Arctic-Circle remote. Each year several million tons of ore are blasted loose and hauled to a port that is free of ice for only three months each year. From there the ore is shipped to blast furnaces in Europe, where it is turned into steel. Working so far north is expensive and dangerous. During the winter, temperatures routinely reach negative forty degrees (measured in either Fahrenheit or Celsius). Machinery is kept running twenty-four hours a day because it is extremely difficult to restart after it cools down. At the camp where the mine workers are housed, two huge generators keep everyone alive. The output of these generators is so important that one is always on standby and two more are stored in reserve. If for some reason, despite all these precautions, all power is lost, the camp must be abandoned within three hours; otherwise its residents would die. When workers drive the two and a half hours from their camp to the port at Milne Inlet, they are required to take a survival kit and enough fuel to last four days. The risk is that a vehicle will break down or a blizzard will make travel impossible. In an extreme arctic blizzard, you can't see your hand held out at arm's length.[1]

Understanding how challenging it is to live and work north of the Arctic Circle shifts the way many of us think of wilderness. We tend to think of wilderness as a metaphorical place of renewal and refreshment, a place where we go to retreat from life's antagonisms. It's a bit harder for us to imagine that when we think of working in negative forty degrees.

The wilderness of the ancient Near East wasn't cold, but neither was it hospitable. When Moses and his people were finally able to leave Egypt, they were not headed to a spa. They were trading violent oppression for the vulnerability of a place where crops wouldn't grow and where water was hard to find. In the last chapter we focused on the story of God rescuing Israel's descendants. Now we turn to their time in the wilderness.

It is precisely because making your way through the wilderness can be such a demanding experience that it can also be deeply formative. In such times and places, people put off old selves and take on new ones. It's in this transformative setting that God gives Israel's children the law. These two things—being freed from slavery and receiving a set of conduct codes—might seem antithetical, like gaining weight while setting a personal best marathon time. How can freedom be gained when law is added? The reality is that these two movements are held together by the larger drama of God's saving work. The priestly role set out for Abraham's descendants in Genesis required them to be a certain sort of people. Priests everywhere are required to go through formational training. Israel is too.

God saves Israel. God sets Israel free. But this freedom isn't a negative freedom, as it would be if they were just freed from some constraint. Israel's freedom is positive, a freedom *for* a better way of being. The solution to the injustice of Egypt and to the universal slavery it represents is a new community—one not governed by the whims of a dictator or protected by a visible fighting force. It is a community governed and protected by God. A key moment in the story of the exodus comes when the whole traveling nation is gathered around Mount Sinai. Here's how it is introduced in Exodus 19:4-6: "You have seen what I did to the Egyptians, and how I bore you on eagles' wings and brought you to myself. Now therefore, if you obey my voice and keep my covenant, you shall be my treasured possession out of all the peoples. Indeed, the whole earth is mine, but you shall be for me a priestly kingdom and a holy nation." The point is this: God liberated Israel from the Egyptians and now wants the people to obey his voice and to keep the covenant. Salvation from domination is for service to God's mission to bless the world.

At one point in my theological studies I decided to visit the places where some of these biblical stories took place. Finding money to travel isn't easy for a graduate student, so my travel came at the expense of some just-about-necessary repairs to my car. It had some electrical problems. If I didn't drive the thing regularly, the battery would die. Occasionally the horn would spontaneously honk. I'd be in traffic, and the horn, obeying some

whim of its own, would blast away. It made me jumpy, but I tried
to be cool. My car needed help, but my hands and feet needed to
connect with the land in which these ancient stories took place.
So I apologized to my (somewhat) faithful car and joined a group
traveling to the Middle East.

One of the things I found, and hadn't thought much about
before, was that the wilderness of the Sinai Peninsula and the
southern part of the modern state of Israel is mostly desert. It's
rocky. The terrain is brown-gray and steep in places. Wadis, or
little canyons, cut through the hill country with an almost unde-
cipherable complexity. The trails are used more by animals than
by people. Shepherds still herd their animals through these hills,
trying to find any forage left after the brief rains. Shepherds water
their animals from secret springs. This desert country is also a
place where the military trains, and where nuclear reactors and
weapons research centers sit relatively undisturbed. This rough
country, which stretches down into North Africa, is the birthplace
of the Torah. As one of my guides put it, this is the land of the
shepherd, not the land of the farmer. Biblically, it is also a place of
trial and judgment, which is to say—again—a place of formation.

In this sort of a landscape, following the wrong path can get
you lost. A misstep can mean injury, and confusion can be devastating. This is probably the type of place that prompts phrases like
"paths of righteousness" (Psalm 23:3, note). Life here is pinched
between survival and extinction. In Psalm 42 the poet describes
his desire for God as a deer longing for the cool refreshment of
flowing streams. In Psalm 23:1-3 we read:

> The LORD is my shepherd, I shall not want.
>   He makes me lie down in green pastures;
> he leads me beside still waters;
>   he restores my soul.
> He leads me in right paths
>   for his name's sake.

The divine leading that the poet has in mind comes through the law. Think of another famous psalm, Psalm 19, which says, "The law of the LORD is perfect, reviving the soul" (v. 7). The law was a blessing. How else would we know how to live in line with the way God created the world? How else would we find wholeness? The law, or the Torah, as it's also called, marks out the path and charts a way through the wilderness.

Enslaved Israel was set free for a purpose, and this purpose required a structured community life. This was intended to form them as a people capable of mediating between God and the rest of creation. In Galatians, Paul describes the law as a tutor or a guardian on duty before Jesus appeared (Galatians 3:24-25). The law was meant to ensure that the sort of injustice that Abraham's descendants experienced in Egypt was not perpetuated in Israel. In fact, we read in Deuteronomy 23 that a slave who escaped from another land was not to be returned. The person was to be allowed to settle in a town in Israel. The law also includes an extension of the environmental ethic begun in the creation story. In Genesis the earth is declared good, and human creatures are told to till and keep it. Leviticus 25 tells us that every seventh year was to be a year of rest for the land. In the same chapter we read, "The land shall not be sold in perpetuity, for the land is mine; with me you are but aliens and tenants" (v. 23). Writer Wendell Berry, a farmer himself, likes to use the old word **usufruct** to describe this concept. The term is a little clunky, but it refers to the legal right a person is given to make use of someone else's property.[2] Israel's job was to show the world what it was like to be a good tenant.

The biblical account of the law sprawls through Exodus, Leviticus, and Deuteronomy. It's a big chunk of text. One way to be more concrete in our thinking about it is to speak of its core, the Ten Commandments. The Ten Commandments, also known as the Decalogue, are a two-sided set of guidelines. One side deals with how we relate to God, and the other with how we relate to our fellow creatures. In Matthew 22, Jesus says that the greatest commandment is to love God and to love one's neighbor. He's referencing the two sides of this list and referring directly to Deuteronomy 6:5 and Leviticus 19:18. If sin distorts relationships, the law is intended to return some measure of good order.

Moses led Israel during their wilderness wanderings. Near the end of his life, recorded in Deuteronomy, he gave a telling description of how Torah was intended to work: "See, I have set before you today life and prosperity, death and adversity. If you obey the commandments of the LORD your God that I am commanding you today, by loving the LORD your God, walking in his ways, and observing his commandments, decrees, and ordinances, then you shall live and become numerous, and the LORD your God will bless you in the land that you are entering to possess" (Deuteronomy 30:15-16).

For ancient Israel, the law was a symbol of their place in God's economy. Unlike the way we sometimes think of the law as making us feel guilty, Israel viewed it as a gift from God. The law was something to celebrate. Judaism has a long tradition of expressing joy for the gift of Torah. Even their old men, gray beards and all, sometimes dance and celebrate it. We would do well to be jubilant with them, for it's in the tradition of Torah that Jesus shows us paths of wholeness in wild and perilous places.

SANCTIFYING THE STUFF OF EARTH

God formed Israel's children through the law but also through worship. To enable corporate worship, they built a moveable structure known as the tabernacle. They built it using the finest stuff they had, which meant it was stuff from their former Egyptian neighbors. It sounds odd, but early Christian theologians found this story to be a helpful allegory for a challenge they faced in the early days of the faith.

These Christian thinkers were doing their best to describe the faith in terms that made sense to their neighbors. We call the early theologians who worked at this **apologists.** Justin Martyr (100–165) might be the best example. He was a philosopher before he became a Christian and continued to wear a philosopher's uniform after his conversion. He believed that in Christianity he had found the true philosophy. It's not surprising that he would become famous for saying, "Whatever things were rightly said among all men, are the property of us Christians." Apologists like Justin used terms and ideas borrowed from the Greek philosophical tradition. They did this liberally.

Other Christian leaders thought this was dangerous. They thought it was confusing the truth of the faith with the idolatry of pagan philosophy. "What has Athens to do with Jerusalem?" asked one of these critics, a former lawyer and important Christian leader named Tertullian (155–240). The apologists responded with a reference drawn from the story of the exodus. In Exodus 12 we read that when the Israelites left the region of their captivity, they "plundered the Egyptians" (v. 36). It was this stuff—jewelry, fine fabrics, precious metals—that was used in the creation of the tabernacle. Early Christian theologians who relied heavily on the Greek philosophical tradition—people like Justin Martyr, Origen, and Augustine, to name just three—thought this little line served as a good model. Just as Israel could find a holy use for these material goods, so Christians should feel free to make use of wider knowledge, especially non-Christian philosophy.

For the wilderness-dwelling Israelites, the most immediate use of this plunder was the creation of the tabernacle. The biblical account begins in Exodus 25, where God instructs Moses to request a material offering from the Israelites to create a sanctuary so God could "dwell among them" (v. 8). Moses gathers gold, silver, bronze, colored cloth, tanned animal skins, special stones, and so on. This stuff would symbolize God's presence.

The important thing to recognize, however, was that the "thing" symbolized by the tabernacle was not absent. We sometimes make symbolic memorials for loved ones who are no longer with us. I have a friend who keeps a piece of the fence from his grandparents' property. The property is no longer in the family. The symbolism of the tabernacle didn't work that way. It was a sign of something that *was* present—present but not clearly perceptible. We can touch, smell, see, and hear the stuff of this earth, but we can't directly perceive God. We need signs.

Augustine is known for describing a **sacrament** as "a visible sign of an invisible grace." The word *sacrament* doesn't show up in our Bibles, but the sense of it is certainly present here, in the creation of the tabernacle. Here, visible things, material things, earthy things are fashioned in such a way that they signify the gracious presence of God. This concept of sacramental presence is deeply important to Christian spirituality. God's presence was signaled throughout the wilderness wanderings by pillars of smoke and fire, then through the tabernacle, and later through the temple. Eventually, God's presence would be signaled by the earthy stuff of Jesus himself.

Part of this formational matrix of symbols and laws is the practice of offering sacrifice. As we read in Leviticus 4, when a priest sinned and violated the law, he was to bring a bull, lay his hands on its head, and slaughter it. If the whole community sinned, a representative elder would perform a similar ritual. If a ruler sinned, he would offer a male goat. Ordinary people would bring a female goat or sheep. If they couldn't afford that, they could bring two doves or even just some flour. Any animal offered had to be a good specimen. This wasn't a way to get rid of unwanted livestock. The whole arrangement demonstrated the importance of the law and reminded Israel of God's grace. It was a form of **atonement**. Sacrifices restored the relationship of a sinful people with God. You can think of this as "at-one-ment." The death of an animal or the burnt offering of grain symbolized the seriousness. Knowing what we do about Jesus, our ears should be ringing with the echoes of his life as we read this part of the biblical text. These institutions are all prototypes of the life and ministry of Jesus.

A FREE GOD AND FREE CREATURES

Emerging from the wilderness, Israelite spies venture into the land where they are to settle. They cross the Jordan and slip into Canaan from the west. The story is told in Numbers 13–14. The problem is, the place is already occupied, and occupied by pretty intimidating folks. The infiltrators report feeling like grasshoppers in the presence of the hulking locals. When the people of Israel hear this report, they are shaken—well, shaken first, and then angry. They howl in despair and say, "Would that we had died in the land of Egypt! Or would that we had died in this wilderness!" (Numbers 14:2). The complaints go on, but you get the point already. God, the parent who arranged this fine little wilderness vacation, seems not a little offended. God says to Moses, "How long will this people despise me? And how long will they refuse to believe in me, in spite of all the signs that I have done among them? I will strike them with pestilence and disinherit them, and I will make of you a nation greater and mightier than they" (vv. 11-12).

This is strong stuff. God is going to kill them off and start over with Moses. But the text gets even weirder. Moses argues with God. He points out that killing the whole group would look bad. He recalls God's "steadfast love." He asks the divine Liberator to rethink. God does just that.

What do we make of this? Can God be influenced by human beings? Does the mind of God change? Can God and human creatures both be free? Another famous passage in the Old Testament raises similar questions. In 1 Samuel 15, God rejects Saul as Israel's king. Verses 11 and 35 suggest that God "regretted" making Saul king. Some translations even say that God "repented." The question is made even more complicated by verse 29, sandwiched between these two references to God's regret, in which Samuel says that God isn't like a human and can't have a change of mind!

Regretting something means thinking through the idea that, had we done things differently, things would have turned out better. Is that what's happening in 1 Samuel? When some theologians run into these questions, they set up a dichotomy between two broad forms of thinking known as **monergism** and **synergism**. Monergism is a perspective that suggests God is the all-determining agent. The strength of this is that it safeguards God's grace. If it were otherwise—if you could somehow compel God to do things—then your salvation would seem to be the result of your good work. You might have forced God's hand. Synergism, on the other hand, suggests that the way history unfolds, either on a grand scale or just on the scale of your afternoon, is not the result of one (*mono-*) actor. It's the combined (*syn-*) result of a divine actor and free creatures. The strength of the synergist perspective is that it recognizes the genuine freedom we feel. We are guilty when we sin because we could have done something else. In some theological conversations you'll hear people use less generic language to speak about what is essentially the same distinction. They'll talk about **Calvinism** in place of monergism and **Arminianism** in place of synergism. We will unpack those two terms later. For now, though, it's worth knowing that when it comes to describing the relationship of the freedom of God and freedom of human creatures, Calvinists emphasize God's control, while Arminians focus on human freedom.

In recent years this discussion has expanded to include a perspective called **open theism**. This view is a more radical derivative of the synergistic, or Arminian, perspective. Those who hold this view believe that since the details of the future are not wholly determined by God, they are not fixed, and therefore are not known by God as anything more than possibilities. This would mean that God could regret making Saul a king precisely because God did not know what he would do. Saul was a free agent. On the surface, this view seems to suggest that God is not **omniscient**, or all-knowing. However, those who advocate for this position, like Anabaptist pastor and theologian Gregory Boyd, argue that they still do believe God knows everything. It's just that the future isn't a thing to be known. Early in his book *God of the Possible*, Boyd writes, "My fundamental thesis is that the classical theological tradition became misguided when . . . it defined God's perfection in static, timeless terms."[3] Why shouldn't we think of a perfect being as one who responds to changes in the situation? Boyd does not believe that God can't determine anything. God does make certain promises and prophecies, which locks some of the future in place. But part of the future remains open because God grants freedom to creatures. Open theism is helpful in the way it draws our attention, once again, to the text of Scripture itself. It pushes us to reread passages that we thought we understood. It helps us see our previous assumptions in a new light and allows us to consider new possibilities for our relationship with our Creator. That said, to the extent that it depends on a metaphysical claim about the future, open theism can feel a bit like a leap into the theoretical ether.

It's tempting to try to find some neat compromise in this debate. It would be nice if we could say that these different ways of talking about God are really claiming the same thing. I don't think they are, and I think many of us aren't very consistent in how we talk about this fundamental aspect of God. We often talk about the moral or devotional life as though things were determined entirely by us—then switch when we begin talking about suffering or death. When we get into those deep waters, we say things like "God called him home," or "It must have been her time." The danger of this sort of incoherence is that it can make the whole faith look like a series of nice things we say to ourselves to get through the moment. Yes, religion can appear to function like an "opium of the people," as Karl Marx claimed. I know more than a few students and parishioners who have been disillusioned by this sort of intellectual inattentiveness.

As I've lived with this question and read fairly widely on it, I've come to think that part of the problem is the way we frame things. We think of God causing something and a human causing something as mutually exclusive. I don't see how one can read the Bible and get the impression that individual human choices aren't significant. On the other hand, to speak of human and divine causation as though they are two equal influences to be combined, like ingredients in a cake, doesn't seem to honor the great and fearful distinction between Creator and creation. The thing is, we don't have the language or the intellectual categories to ever really describe how a divine Creator interacts with creation. Much of theological language is analogical, right? Therefore I don't see any contradiction in speaking of the reality of divine *and* human freedom. The existence of one need not eliminate the other. Both can be real and true.

There is no problem with speaking of our daily activities as free choices. You could have a beef or veggie burger; you could wear a vest or a hoodie. Saul could have led Israel with integrity. The ancient Israelites could have made a decision to trust in God's provision instead of being bowled over by fear. God has given human creatures freedom. And that is without doubt a good thing. What we are *not* free to do, however, is entirely avoid behaving inappropriately toward ourselves and others. That is not within the scope of our freedom. If freedom is doing what we *want*, the problem is that we don't always *want* to do the best things. We are not free, in and of ourselves, to live peaceably as the logic of creation, the Word, would beckon us to do. For that we need and have been given outside intervention—intervention we can accept or, like Israel on the cusp of entering the land, intervention to which we can turn our backs.

8

GIVE US *a* KING

Providence

So what, in loving God, do I love?
—**Augustine**

To be alive is to be vulnerable to being dead. I haven't yet found a way in which that claim isn't true. Being alive means we are not invincible. It means we are never in total control. Sometimes vulnerability is quite wonderful, like when someone you love deeply tells you that they also love you. If you forced the statement, it would not be the same. Vulnerability can also be terrifying, however—like when someone you don't trust has power over you, or when a vehicle is about to plow into you and your bike.

For several years I attended a little Anglican church just a block off Main Street in a small town. It was a charming and simple congregation. Many of the people who participated in the church did so as a respite from larger, more heavily programmed churches in the area. After each service our little Anglican group would have an after-party with tea and toast. The physical property was simple too. Besides the main building, which was no bigger than many houses in the neighborhood, there was only a little shed, where plywood versions of the holy family and their supporting cast stayed in the off season. There was no room for them in the church building itself.

At the back of the sanctuary, behind the mismatched wooden benches, were stacks of red prayer books. They were well worn and small enough that you could fit one in the pocket of your jeans. Sometimes we would use the old books for a prayer service. That was where I first encountered a prayer that went something like this:

> Almighty and everlasting God, in whom we live and move and
>   have our being;
> We, your needy creatures, give you our humble praises,
>   for your preservation of us from the beginning of our lives
>   to this day, and especially for having delivered us from the
>   dangers of the past night.
> For these your mercies, we bless and magnify your glorious
>   Name . . . Amen.

This is the sort of prayer I always have to read twice. Each time I do I'm struck by the bit about the "dangers of the past night." What did the author have in mind? What about the many people who have prayed these words—what's been on their minds? I doubt that a modern prayer book would include such a prayer. Many of us aren't as aware of nighttime dangers as were previous generations. Now we can turn on lights if there's an odd noise or call for help on a cell phone. We modern folks don't like to think about our vulnerability. Yet when that prayer passes through my lips, the stories of people I know who have been terrorized in the night roll through my mind. God knows we are still vulnerable.

As much as vulnerability is a part of our human experience, so is trying to avoid it. Think of our desire for weather forecasts and our frustration that they aren't 100 percent accurate. Sometimes when my wife and I would walk home from the church with the little red prayer books, we would pass a house with a sign that read THIS HOME PROTECTED BY A .44 MAGNUM. It was a bit of a joke, I guess. Many of the houses on the block advertised that they were protected by electronic security systems. This universal reality—that being alive means we are vulnerable—is one of the things that link us to ancient Israel. In fact, it's one way to understand Israel's desire for a king.

A WARRING PEOPLE

The ancient tribes of Israel settled the land without a monarchy in place. God's intention was to lead the people in an immediate sense, relying on the gifts of judges, prophets, and priests. When Israel needed defending, an ad hoc force would be raised. One example is the story of Gideon in Judges 6–7. God called him to protect the people from invaders, but Gideon was doubtful. He asked God for some signs. God obliged. Gideon was convinced and set about gathering an army, only to have God send most of the men home. The rationale, as God told Gideon, was this: "The troops with you are too many for me to give the Midianites into their hand. Israel would only take the credit away from me, saying, 'My own hand has delivered me'" (Judges 7:2). God wanted it to be clear that the people were under divine protection. As with any community, the environment would make them vulnerable. God wanted their response to be one of trust. Think of the way Joshua "conquers" Jericho. It's the same dynamic. The war stories in this part of the Bible aren't about war in any modern sense. The lesson is never that the Israelite tribes should start a national defense program or have a standing army to deter invaders.

It is impossible to read these stories and not ask questions about their moral significance. Just as violence can be motivated by secular agendas, so it can be motivated by faith. Therefore, it's important to remember that Christian thinking about war isn't only based on this part of Scripture. We also rely on the later witness of the Prophets, the teaching of Jesus, the letters and example of the early church. The connection between Christian morality and the life of ancient Israel isn't direct. In fact, the writers of the New Testament and the theologians who followed tended to apply these texts allegorically. They filtered their moral significance through the life, death, and resurrection of Jesus.

Christians generally approach war from one of two perspectives, advocating either **pacifism** or **just war**. Like everything, the reality is more complex than these neat categories suggest. These get us started, though. Pacifists say that our default should always be peace, even if it means suffering. When it comes to Scripture, pacifism draws its rationale most directly from Jesus, especially his command to love our enemies. In his Sermon on the Mount, Jesus tells his followers to do that and to not retaliate. Pacifists point out that it's hard to imagine loving someone while killing them. They also point out that when Paul speaks of governing authorities, he doesn't seem to think of Christians getting involved. Early Christians did not generally serve in the military or get enthusiastic about nationalist projects. They were a minority people in a large, sprawling empire. They had little political power and little stake in the empire's success.

This changed over the next few centuries, as churches grew and more people from higher social positions joined the faith. The Christian community is a living thing, and it was not long before the ethic of avoiding participation in war tilted in the other direction. The most notable proponent of the more accommodationist view was Augustine. In the early fifth century, Augustine wrote a massive book called *The City of God*. My English copy runs well over one thousand pages. The situation that prompted the book was the weakening of the Roman Empire in the West and the possibility that Christianity might have been one of the causes for the decline. In the book, Augustine reflects on the forceful ways the empire tried to unify people of different cultures. He bemoans the misery caused by war. Yet he writes, "But the wise man, they say, will wage just wars. Surely, however, if he remembers that he is a human being, he will be much readier to deplore the fact that he is under the necessity of waging even just wars."[1] Augustine is far from celebrating war, but his description of wars that were justified has proven influential.

Those who advocate for Christian participation in war believe that, although war should never be celebrated as a good, certain wars can be justified. They don't think of postbiblical wars as holy wars like Israel's, but they do see these ancient conflicts as a demonstration that God doesn't categorically oppose killing. They also point out that Jesus interacted with soldiers and didn't tell them all to quit their jobs. Advocates of just war are quick to point to Romans 13 as well. In that passage Paul argues that governing authorities bear the sword for a valid reason. He says that governments serve God as they "execute wrath on the wrongdoer" (v. 4). In theological conversation, a war is said to be justified if the following are true:

- It has a just cause.
- It is a last resort.
- It is initiated by a proper authority.
- It has a good intention.
- It has a reasonable chance of success.
- Its goal is proportional to its means.

Notice that these criteria rule out retribution, rebellion, and doomed battles fought for honor. In addition to these criteria for entering a conflict, ongoing participation can only be justified if noncombatants are not targeted and if the destructive power used is in proportion to the good intended. The idea is to cause the minimum amount of suffering required to achieve the goal.

This tradition of justifying warfare has been carried by the main body of the church since somewhere around the fifth century. At the same time, pacifism has been practiced by some monastic orders and reform movements. In the sixteenth century, pacifism was embraced by most of the Anabaptist Reformers. Along with Quakers and some charismatic groups, their spiritual heirs remain the most notable advocates of that tradition today.

The most vexing challenge for pacifists and just war proponents alike is how to deal with violent powers that harm the innocent. Does going to war and killing make the overall situation better? Is it more Christlike to simply suffer with the innocent? We have to admit that Christians have sometimes used their faith to rationalize violence when the only real goal was to advance the interests of their own people. Such causes wear the mask of faith, but they are patently contrary to a faith that embraces all nations and all peoples. Both pacifists and just war advocates can resist the ways nations organize civic life to cultivate an unquestioning belief in the righteousness of any nation.

Just war adherents who are morally serious and pacifists who care about the well-being of those outside their community are not as far apart as it might first appear. Both see peace as a goal, both realize that armed conflict can often be prevented by addressing root causes, both acknowledge the necessity of some form of policing, both regret the massive resources poured into the machinery of war, and both weep over the generational trauma initiated by participation in war. Christians of all stripes know that war is not to be celebrated. It is not something that we should take pride in or love or something we should aspire to or sentimentalize. A quick way to test our thinking about violence generally is to imagine that those we love most are on the other side. How then would we engage our "enemy"?

One of the contemporary church's key challenges is its disunity. We refer to the work of healing this rupture as **ecumenism**. It's tempting, when thinking about the morality of war, to say that various parts of the Christian community have differing gifts, in this case some to witness to Christ's peace and some to bear the sword of justice. This model—thinking of differences as gifts—is generally helpful; however, it can also be one more way that we embrace individualism and evade the hard work that unity requires. On this issue it is particularly helpful for us to have a clear vision of the center to which we're all drawn. From there we can discern where love and the fractured state of the world might require exceptions.

With respect to the question of participation in war, the center is not the wars of Israel. The center is the peace of the Incarnate Word. It is Isaiah's prophecy that the weapons of war will be reworked into farm tools. Christians witness to this future now by being skeptical that violence can fix things or that it is the only way to achieve peace. With the poet who wrote Psalm 20, we confess these words: "Some take pride in chariots, and some in horses, but our pride is in the name of the LORD our God" (v. 7). The simple truth is that no amount of power can eliminate our vulnerability to suffering and death. That's something only God can do.

IN THOSE DAYS THERE WAS NO KING

Throughout the book of Judges, God calls a variety of—you guessed it—*judges* to lead and defend Israel. There is Deborah and the infamous strongman Samson. There is Jael, who saved Israel by hammering a stake through the head of a napping king. In addition to these sorts of leaders were the priests. The priests, members of the tribe of Levi, didn't have a specified territory, as the other tribes did. Instead, they were spread out; their job was to tell the old stories and teach the ways of Torah.

Things did not go well for tribal Israel. One of the keys to understanding the book of Judges is this simple line: "The Israelites did what was evil in the sight of the LORD." These words are repeated as a part of a cycle: Israel would turn away from the law; they would be oppressed by enemies; they would plead with God for help; God would provide a leader to defend them; things would go well for a time; then the cycle would be repeated. More simply, the cycle was one of sin, judgment, and repentance.

The narrative of Judges ends with a story showing the nation's corruption. The main characters are a Levite and his concubine. It is a hideous story. It is a "text of terror," as biblical scholar Phyllis Trible refers to it. The story begins in the first verse of Judges 19: "In those days, when there was no king in Israel . . ." It goes on to describe how a Levite had taken a woman from Bethlehem as his concubine. The woman wasn't happy in his company and so returned to her family. After several months the Levite decided he would try to woo her back. He goes and is successful, but ends up staying longer than planned. Because they leave late, the two are forced to spend the night in an unfamiliar town. They are taken in by an old man who insists that it would be a bad idea for them to spend the night in the town square. Indeed, it would have been.

Late that night there is a pounding on the door. Some of the city's men are there. They urge the old man to turn his visitor out so that they can have sex with him. The old man will have none of it, but to keep the men at bay he sends out his daughter and the Levite's concubine. "Ravish them and do whatever you want to them," he says, but he insists that they don't rape his male guest. The men gang-rape the Levite's concubine through the night. In the morning the Levite finds her lying in the doorway. "Get up," he says, "we are going." She doesn't move. The Levite ties the dead woman to his donkey and leaves. When he reaches his home, he cuts the woman's body into pieces and sends them throughout the land of Israel. Messengers tell the story, and the tribes of Israel erupt in violence. In the last verse of Judges 21, the story concludes with these words: "In those days there was no king in Israel; all the people did what was right in their own eyes."

This story is one that Phyllis Trible features in her book *Texts of Terror*. In the book, the illustration related to this story shows a headstone engraved with the words "An Unnamed Woman, Concubine from Bethlehem."[2] Trible points out that even as this story speaks to the time of the judges, it speaks to our time as well. She writes, "Misogyny belongs to every age, including our own. Violence and vengeance are not just characteristics of a distant, pre-Christian past; they infect the community of the elect to this day. Woman as object is still captured, betrayed, raped, tortured, murdered, dismembered, and scattered. To take to heart this ancient story, then, is to confess its present reality."[3] For Trible this is not the only such text within the covers of the Bible. There are many.

Trible is a leading figure in **feminist biblical interpretation**. Her approach has been very influential. Trible analyzes Scripture with special attention to the way it portrays women. She draws readers to the stories of Hagar, an enslaved woman used, abused, and rejected; Tamar, a princess raped and put aside; the Levite's concubine; and the daughter of Jephthah, a virgin killed and sacrificed. Trible wants her readers to notice more than just the usual heroes of the biblical stories. She wants them to see the women who get trampled. Of course not all feminist readings of the Bible are the same. Some women of color, for example, place greater emphasis on the story of Hagar. Hagar's status as a slave, the way she stands outside the privileged kinship network of Abraham and Sarah, her lonely struggle to provide for her son—all these factors connect with Hagar's stirring experience of God's provision. Such interpretations ask us to be conscious of the ways in which traditional readings of the Bible have served to support the privilege of certain members of society. The story of the Levite's concubine is a good example because, although it tells the story of a horrifically abused woman, its literary function is to demonstrate the need for a (male) monarch.

THOSE WHO BEAR THE SWORD

In the beginning of 1 Samuel we meet a woman who deeply desires a child but has been unable to conceive. Her name is Hannah, and she prays with verve and conviction until God grants her a son. She names him Samuel and dedicates him for God's work. Samuel becomes Israel's judge and eventually tries to establish his own sons in the same role. Although Samuel is faithful, his sons are not. Israel's sense of vulnerability and moral ferment converge in their request to the aging Samuel: "Give us a king to govern us" (1 Samuel 8:6). The request would seem to be the undoing of the whole test-plot project. How could they fulfill their mission by imitating nations?

This story prompts several questions for modern readers. One is simply how we should think of kings or monarchies generally or even other forms of government, like democracies. If God is the true ruler of the universe, are governments helpful or destructive? In the Romans 13 passage I mentioned earlier, Paul describes governing powers as God's servants. You don't need to worry about them, he suggests, unless you're in the wrong. Paul wrote before the destruction of Jerusalem in 70 CE, before Nero began persecuting Christians, and before the emperor declared himself a god. There's another picture of a government in the Bible, one that was written after those things happened. It's from Revelation 13. There, John depicts governing powers as a vicious, imperial beast. It seems that both these possibilities exist. Governmental power can be used to restrain evil or to consume people and cultures in despotic self-interest. Israel hoped for the former; they got some of that, but also much of the latter.

In a surprising turn, God tells Samuel, "Listen to the voice of the people . . . they have not rejected you, but they have rejected me from being king over them" (1 Samuel 8:7). The rejection of divine rule fits the pattern of Israel's lack of trust ever since they walked out of Egypt and into the wilderness. Give the people what they want, God says, but before you do, let them know how bad it will be. Samuel tells them a king would take their children, their fields, their vineyards, their olive orchards, their servants, their donkeys, and their flocks. "You will cry out because of your king," God says through Samuel (v. 18).

We realize here, if we haven't already, that one of the key characteristics of the Almighty is a willingness to **condescend**. God stoops to connect with nearsighted creatures. God "meets us where we are," as we sometimes say. John Calvin described God as "lisping," in the way one alters one's voice to speak to a child. The God we encounter in the Bible is the stooping, lisping Creator. Not to jump too far ahead in the biblical story, but we'll see that God uses this fraught role of a temporal sovereign as an opportunity for self-revelation. Jesus takes on this role—he's mockingly called the "King of the Jews"—and then turns it inside out and upside down. Jesus replaces the self-serving character of monarchs with the other-oriented perspective of a voluntary servant. Jesus gets rid of the elitist character of monarchs and rides into Jerusalem on a humble work animal. Jesus abandons the hierarchical, lording manner of monarchs and replaces it with the approach of one who holds power for the good of others.

That is all compelling and true, but it is built on the stories of kings like Saul, whom Samuel initially anoints, and David, who takes his place. The troubling connotations of monarchical power notwithstanding, David is described in Acts 13 as a man after God's own heart. David's poetry makes up much of the Psalms. This, even though he had one of his loyal soldiers killed so he could rape the man's wife with impunity. The first verse of the New Testament even identifies Jesus as "the son of David" (Matthew 1:1). The concept of a sovereign monarch is incorporated into God's redemptive work.

A monarch, just like an ambassador or a CEO or a president, speaks and acts on behalf of a whole community. In theological lingo we sometimes speak of this as **corporate solidarity**. This is where the identity of a whole people is defined by the speech and actions of one person. It's hard for many modern people to fathom such a thing. We are individuals, and we can't imagine being praised or judged for the work someone else does. We get riled up at the idea that we might have to pay someone else's debt or be held responsible for someone else's mistakes. Reading Scripture is a cross-cultural experience, however, and the pattern of corporate solidarity runs throughout. Adam represents all of humanity. Israel is represented by their king. Both of these prefigure the work of Jesus. In Jesus is found the entirety of Israel, and in Jesus is found all of Adam's race.

Before closing this chapter, I should mention one more thing. It's something the above discussion of solidarity might have already suggested. I've presented Israel's request for a king as contrary to the role God had planned for Israel. The book of 1 Samuel makes that reality clear. Nevertheless, being contrary to God's will does not mean the development is beyond the scope of God's sovereignty. If you flip back to Deuteronomy 17 you'll notice that there are laws given for kings. Kings shouldn't exalt themselves over other members of the community, and nor should they ignore Torah. The king was even required to have an official copy of the Law close at hand. Israelite kings were supposed to behave differently from their international peers. They were not to stockpile too much money or too many horses or wives. This all fits the pattern in which God's power is used to keep the mission going even when the human covenant partners fail. We will see much more of this.

9

DO JUSTICE
and LOVE KINDNESS

Faithfulness

Let me look up at your light, whether from afar or from the depths. Teach me how to seek you, and show yourself to me when I seek. For I cannot seek you unless you teach me how, and I cannot find you unless you show yourself to me.
—**Anselm of Canterbury**

I received the rolled-up diploma in the University of Toronto's magnificent Convocation Hall. The building is a copper-domed rotunda inspired by the Sorbonne in Paris. Historically, to be a "doctor" was to be recognized as a teacher. My classmates and I were awarded our degrees by a man gowned in blue and gold who conferred the credentials in Latin. That all has grand connotations.

In reality, holding a doctoral degree in theology today correlates with low financial prospects and strained familial relationships. I had decided to pursue the degree after my studies in Virginia because I wanted to learn more about the connection between theology and politics and because I thought the additional study might equip me to serve some part of the Christian community. If I had hoped that such studies would provide additional social status, I was badly mistaken. I once tried to explain my field of study to an accounts manager at a bank. "Theology," he said, "that's in the medical field, isn't it?"

Studying in Toronto was like a multiyear treasure hunt. The collection of theological books was spread over the libraries of six or so affiliated schools. You would enter the name of a volume into the computer, and it would tell you if it was in the university's collection (it always was) and which library had the book. Then you would have to scamper across several city blocks, decipher the library's map, and meander through the stacks to figure out how the letter-number combinations jumped from one shelf to the next.

Having visited each library, I quickly developed an affinity for one in particular. It was a nineteenth-century stone building rimming a courtyard with a perfect lawn and reflecting pool. It had a fireplace and dark oak study carrels. I would study there whenever possible. One of the stories I came across between those oak panels was of a child born in the fourth century to a leading Roman family. The child was born in Gaul, and according to legend, he was once found in his cradle with a swarm of bees covering his face. When the bees were chased away, a drop of honey was left on his mouth. The little one would be known as Ambrose (339–97), and he would become famous for his honeyed tongue. Young Ambrose studied literature, law, and rhetoric in Rome. He began a political career but then, in a surprising turn, was called to be the bishop of Milan. This was not his goal; in fact, he wasn't even baptized. Nevertheless, he was eventually convinced of the call. Ambrose began studying theology in earnest and took up correspondence with some of the best theological minds of his day.

Ambrose's appointment happened during a time of intense theological disagreement. The issue under dispute was how we should speak about Jesus, the Son of God and second person of the Trinity. Ambrose was of the opinion that the Son was eternal and no less divine than the Father. On the other side of the issue were the Arians, who believed that the Son of God was created in time. Ambrose developed a reputation of being able to disagree without being pugnacious. He would become one of the four theologians recognized as "doctors" of the church in the West. Augustine, Gregory the Great, and Jerome were the other three. It was Ambrose's deft preaching and biblical exegesis that eased some of Augustine's hesitations about the faith. Augustine observed Ambrose up close, even remarking that when Ambrose read, he did something that was considered odd at the time: he didn't say or even mouth the words. In the Eastern Church, John Chrysostom, Gregory of Nazianzus, and Basil the Great had similar honors to the four from the West. Being a doctor in this sense meant that they were considered trustworthy interpreters of Scripture.

Part of Ambrose's interpretation of Scripture was his deep commitment to justice and care for the poor. It was one of the things that made him so influential. When he was first ordained, he gave away most of what he owned and took up a monastic lifestyle. Another event would cement his reputation as a moral force. When the city of Thessalonica revolted against its magistrate, the emperor Theodosius responded with overwhelming force. He treated the city with a cruelty usually reserved for captured enemies, killing thousands. When Ambrose heard about the emperor's actions, he banned him from communion. This was a very clear and very public moral statement. Theodosius had to perform penance to be restored to full fellowship with the church.

The story illustrates both Ambrose's sense of justice and the power of a bishop in relation to an emperor. Ambrose wasn't perfect: his views of Jews and other non-Christians would make us cringe. But he did demonstrate a penchant for justice and care for the poor at a key point in the history of Christianity. His convictions weren't novel. Early Christians gave sacrificially to care for the poor. The rough contours of the way of life defined in the Old Testament made space for outsiders and mandated care for widows and orphans. It was the prophet Micah who famously said that even when the sacrificial system was up and running, what God really wanted was for people "to do justice, and to love kindness, and to walk humbly with your God" (Micah 6:8).

THE PSALMS AND THE LIFE OF FAITH

This stream of justice, which sustained both Ambrose and Micah, carries several biblical claims about the human person. This brings us back to the part of the theological conversation referred to as theological anthropology. In addition to the things we've said about human creatures according to the early chapters of Genesis, the psalms make a few other things apparent. The psalms exemplify the assumption that human creatures are more than physical entities. Here's the fifth verse of Psalm 42: "Why are you cast down, O my soul, and why are you disquieted within me?" The word *soul* appears six times in this eleven-verse poem. The poet has the clear impression that he is more than a machine for gaining and expending energy. There is something about us that transcends our bodies.

Exactly how we should speak about this "more than" is not a settled matter. Some theologians see a clear answer in 1 Thessalonians 5:23: "May the God of peace himself sanctify you entirely; and may your spirit and soul and body be kept sound and blameless at the coming of our Lord Jesus Christ." The assumption in this passage seems to be that a human is made up of a spirit, a soul, and a body. This is the **trichotomist** perspective. Trichotomists see the spirit as the part of ourselves that connects with God, and the soul as our intellect, will, and personality. However, others don't see this distinction between spirit and soul as terribly important. This is a **dichotomist** perspective. People who see this as the best way to speak about the "more than" think of the human creature simply as being composed of a tangible, material entity and an intangible, inner entity. Either way, the shared conviction that we are more than our bodies is one of the reasons, although certainly not the only one, that Christians believe each human life has inherent worth.

Psalms has done a lot to shape the Christian faith. It contains the most popular parts of the Bible. One of the great gifts of this chunk of Scripture is the permission it gives us to express to God our doubt, pain, and lament. Hear the distress in Psalm 13:1: "How long, O LORD? Will you forget me forever? How long will you hide your face from me?" And hear the exhaustion in Psalm 22:14: "I am poured out like water, and all my bones are out of joint." The power of the psalms comes not only from propositions about God or the life of faith but also from their artistry. This points us to the significance of art in the life of faith and more specifically to its role in worship. These poems have been set to music in many different cultural contexts. The psalms show us that God is big enough to hear our frustration and pain.

This spiritual wisdom is surprising if you think about David's biography. David didn't author all the psalms, but many are attributed to him. Some of David's actions would have gotten the attention of Ambrose, and not in a positive way. David, after all, was the guy who took the foreskins from one hundred men as a gift for the father of his bride. Assuming a vague similarity between ancient and modern men, these fellows would not have given their foreskins to David voluntarily. Nevertheless, what David had—and this is probably why he's praised in the book of Acts—was a deep commitment to serving and trusting God. This is apparent in improbable ways, but none more so than in his military endeavors. In the epic story of his confrontation with the Philistine champion Goliath, recorded in 1 Samuel 17, David's courage is founded on his belief that "the battle is the LORD's." David was obviously outgunned, but he believed that what would move the story of his people forward was ultimately not their own power but God's.

The openness and honesty of the psalms, the reliance upon God that they express, their lyricism—these are all reasons that this book is the most important and ancient of Christian worship resources. Psalms demonstrates another component of our theological anthropology, the fact that the human person is a worshiping creature. To be a human creature is to desire, to love, and to worship. If we don't think about worship too narrowly, we realize it is as natural for us as anything else we do. We naturally position ourselves in relation to things that are bigger than us. We are members of fan clubs and political parties. We offer our bodies to our nations or our sports teams. We give up our individuality and become part of a mass in a crowded concert or a protest march. Our mouths shout about injustice or the greatness of our tribe. We become willing subjects of brands and trends. We give ourselves to things, we are drawn to transcendence—we worship.

Miroslav Volf, a contemporary theologian originally from Croatia, observes that modern culture identifies flourishing with "experiential satisfaction."[1] We assume that life is good when we feel pleasure. What Volf points out, and what many of us have experienced, is that our desire for pleasure is never satisfied. We have infinite desire, but things are finite. Perhaps David himself illustrated this with his pursuit of a married woman, a pursuit of pleasure as an end in itself. Volf observes that without a connection to something bigger, even the best of pleasures will inevitably taste stale.

In contrast to the idea that a good life is skipping from one pleasurable experience to the next, a Christian view says that truly flourishing involves loving God and our neighbors.[2] Our deepest desire and our deepest love find their fulfillment in God and, as Ambrose and innumerable others found, in caring for those creatures who bear God's image. Thus, to cherry-pick a few lines from Psalm 63, we hear the poet saying, "O God, you are my God, I seek you, my soul thirsts for you. . . . Your steadfast love is better than life. . . . So I will bless you as long as I live" (vv. 1, 3-4). More than just a compromised example of the life of faith, David foreshadows the one whose faith would be universally salvific. David is a type of savior, or as we said of Joseph, David is a prototype. By recognizing his dependence on God, David saves Israel from their enemies. The difference between a "type" and the real thing, in this case, is that Jesus makes a difference not just for one nation but for everyone.

FAITH AND WISDOM

David wanted to build a permanent place of worship in Jerusalem, but God wouldn't have it. David was a man of violence. The job would go to Solomon, his son. Like the tabernacle before it, the temple served as a focal point for worship. It was lavish. In addition to serving the tribes of Israel, the temple was a place where foreigners could pray. In his dedication, recorded in 1 Kings, Solomon asks of God that "when a foreigner comes and prays toward this house, then hear . . . and do according to all that the foreigner calls to you, so that all the peoples of the earth may know your name" (8:42-43). The temple was to signify God's global repair mission.

Whatever the purpose of the temple, let's be clear: there was nothing pure about it. It was built with forced labor. It fulfilled

Samuel's warning about the terrible costs of having a king. The temple is just one example of Solomon's devastating capriciousness. The first part of 1 Kings 11 chronicles his errors: he had many foreign wives, he worshiped pagan deities, and he even built sites for worship in their honor. Oddly, Solomon is famous for his wisdom. Large chunks of the First Testament are linked to him, specifically Proverbs, Ecclesiastes, and Song of Solomon. These books, with the addition of Job, are referred to as the **wisdom literature.**

One of the things that make this literature stand out is that these works lack obvious links to the special revelation of the Torah. Think of Proverbs. In the first chapter of the book we read that "Wisdom cries out in the street" (Proverbs 1:20). The working assumption is that wisdom is out there, available to everyone, not contained in one text. Biblical wisdom literature is itself part of a literary tradition that stretches beyond the biblical canon. It's sometimes tempting for Christians to be narrow-minded about these kinds of things. We might be tempted to think that wisdom and other virtues belong uniquely to Christians. Non-Christians just don't get it, we think: they can't understand love, or the workings of the world, or whatever we might be thinking about at that moment. This is the arrogance of fundamentalism.

In reality, even the most narrow-minded and idealistic person of faith believes in wisdom beyond their sacred texts. We do not expect the auto mechanic to consult the Bible in order to fix our car. We do not expect the baker to get all her recipes from the Bible. Experience shows that people of various faiths can agree, at some level, on what constitutes good government and fairness. The question is not whether we acknowledge something like general revelation or wider wisdom but rather how we understand the witness of Scripture in relation to culture's wider wisdom.

Sometimes, broader knowledge clarifies the message of Scripture. The findings of science, however much they are in flux, can help us focus on the Bible's main message. Here's one benign example: In Exodus 17, Moses tells Joshua to gather soldiers and take them into battle. Moses will then stand atop a nearby hill and hold the staff of God. When Moses's hands are held aloft, the men of Israel prevail; when his hands drop, they get their butts kicked. Moses gets tired (you try holding a stick in the air for hours), so two fellows sit him down on a rock and each hold up one of his hands. Then—and here's what I want us to notice— we read that "his hands were steady until the sun set" (Exodus 17:12). Maybe you know intuitively what I'm about to say: the Sun does not set, nor does it "go down," as other translations say. We know it is the Earth that rotates. Yet Exodus says something quite different.

We can probably see our way through this interpretive challenge without breaking a sweat. The writer's point isn't really about how the planets do or don't move in relation to the Sun. The writer is speaking in the terms set by an ancient **cosmology**. A cosmology is a sort of theoretical map of how the Earth works and how the planets and stars relate. Some biblical writers envisioned the Earth to be supported by pillars, which kept it from sinking into water. They believed the Sun and stars moved within a dome, above which more water was stored. The biblical writers used the language and assumptions of a cosmology like this to communicate more important things. The point of the story of Moses's droopy hands is to tell readers about God's power and the special role of the covenant people.

The wider wisdom of science helps focus our reading on what matters most in the text. You'll notice something similar if you carefully compare 2 Samuel 10:18 and 1 Chronicles 19:18. These two verses are about the same battle, but the facts they report don't line up. Reason tells us that both can't be accurate in the details. Again, basic reason points us through the difference to the deeper theme of God's rule and David's faithful response.

In theological conversation, the capacity of human creatures to reason and make observations about our world—the capacity on which science is built—is part of what we call **common grace**. This refers to the gifts God has given to all people. Pick up a copy of *Scientific American* or *National Geographic*, *The Economist* or *Dwell*, and page through it. If you've been too focused on spiritual things to notice the enormous creative and analytical capacity of people generally, you may be missing out on common grace.

The reality of this immense knowledge was hard for me to miss during my doctoral studies in Toronto. Almost every day I walked past the medical buildings, the law school, the engineering building, and so forth. The hub of the library system I burrowed into was a fourteen-story concrete building shaped like a peacock. It held millions of books. Reading theology in such a context was both humbling and thrilling. Paul's speech in Acts 17, with its references to the unknown God of the Athenians and quotations of pagan poets, took on new significance.

This shouldn't be all that surprising. Scripture positions itself in a sort of dialogue with wider wisdom. Wisdom literature gives us the sense that real wisdom is available to those who pay attention. Proverbs 30 and 31 are attributed to two mysterious figures named Agur and Lemuel. There's no solid consensus on who these fellows were, but many think these chapters represent wisdom from beyond Israel. It's also probable that portions of Proverbs 22–24, the "sayings of the wise," make use of older Egyptian sayings. There's also the way 1 Kings 4 describes the abilities of Solomon: "God gave Solomon very great wisdom, discernment, and breadth of understanding as vast as the sand on the seashore, so that Solomon's wisdom surpassed the wisdom of all the people of the east, and all the wisdom of Egypt. He was wiser than anyone else, wiser than Ethan the Ezrahite, and Heman, Calcol, and Darda, children of Mahol; his fame spread throughout all the surrounding nations" (vv. 29-31).

Wisdom surpassing that of Egypt and that of the people of the east? Wiser than anyone else? The writer is mostly trying to tell us how wise Solomon was, but implicitly he is telling us that the others had wisdom too. To say that Solomon is wiser is different from saying the others had nothing to offer.

We must note one more thing before we turn our attention away from Proverbs. This is related to the way Wisdom is personified. Some theologians speak of Wisdom not as human reason or judgment but as God's Self. They sometimes refer to Holy Wisdom, or Sophia. This tradition is strongest in Orthodox circles. In the 1930s the discussion of Sophia caused significant rifts among exiled Russian theologians. The work of Sergei Bulgakov (1871–1944) and Pavel Florensky (1882–1937) was at the center of this controversy. Later scholars, especially feminist theologians, have found their descriptions of Sophia provocative and fertile. Since it is difficult to speak of God in non-gendered terms, the personification of Wisdom as a woman gives some biblical footing for using feminine pronouns in addition to masculine ones.

SUFFERING AND THE LITERATURE OF PROTEST

Wisdom literature is one of the anchor points for philosophy within the Bible itself. There are few places where this is clearer than in the book of Job. Job is a prolonged meditation on suffering. Where Proverbs, and Psalms to some extent, imply that the person who makes wise decisions will prosper, the story of Job explores how this isn't always true. The first verse of the book says Job was "blameless and upright; one who feared God and turned away from evil." Yet Job suffered—a lot. For its original audience, Job probably symbolized the suffering of the exiled Jews. By extension, he stands for the innocent who suffer the world over.

We're talking, of course, about how we understand the reality of suffering. This is a classic philosophical problem, but it's also a basic part of everyone's life of faith. We could tack lots of other stories on to Job's. We could add victims of famine or refugees or those who have been abused. We could add an unending list of good people who have been afflicted by disease or who have lost jobs through no fault of their own. Job's friends give him standard lines, some that are still in circulation today: they believe he must have done something wrong to deserve what he got. This sort of a response is a type of **theodicy**: an explanation for the presence of suffering and evil in God's good world. Arguments like this try to explain suffering. Job is adamant that his friends' explanations don't hold. He is innocent, yet there he sits scratching his sores with a broken piece of pottery, his family destroyed and his wealth gone.

God responds near the end of the book. But God doesn't offer any real explanation, only a description of the gulf between human creatures and the transcendent God. The goodness of the biblical God is not one value in a balanced equation. God supersedes all such equations. Here's the account from chapter 38: "Then the LORD answered Job out of the whirlwind: 'Who is this that darkens counsel by words without knowledge? Gird up your loins like a man, I will question you, and you shall declare to me. Where were you when I laid the foundation of the earth?'" (vv. 1-4). Notice that there is no neat answer that makes suffering all right, no simple calculus of wrong action equaling suffering or suffering always making us better people.

Theologians across the generations have had much to say about this. Augustine, in some of his early work, connected suffering to human freedom. In this vein, suffering is a necessary risk required to realize the greater good of being free creatures. Others have argued that all pain is intended by God as part of some larger project. "Everything happens for a reason," these folks say. I am not convinced. Surely there are *causes* for everything. And surely in some mysterious and powerful way, God is capable of redeeming all things. That is what Paul is getting at when he writes in Romans 8:28 that "all things work together for good for those who love God."

Yet the book of Job offers a counterbalance to the calm, mechanical assurances that everything happens for a reason—and to the assurance of Proverbs, for that matter. Here's one example from Job 24:

> Why are times not kept by the Almighty,
> and why do those who know him never see his days?
> The wicked remove landmarks;
> they seize flocks and pasture them.
> They drive away the donkey of the orphan;
> they take the widow's ox for a pledge.
> They thrust the needy off the road;
> the poor of the earth all hide themselves. (vv. 1-4)

The book of Job thus canonizes questions and ambiguity. Along with the Psalms, the book of Job creates space within the life of faith for questions and doubt. With all of Scripture, these books hold up the importance of justice and kindness. They also add the observation that the Christian call to justice isn't a program for eliminating suffering. We can't read these biblical books and walk away with the sense that we will get through life on our terms. We can't control everything. Things will happen to us and to those we love. Job and the Psalms give us a sense of how we might talk to God anyway.

10

I WILL MAKE
a NEW COVENANT

Anticipation

If we begin to read the Bible as a book of God's hope, then we will find that it is a highly revolutionary and subversive book.
—**Jürgen Moltmann**

U nder David's leadership, Israel was consolidated from a loose collection of tribes to a nation with centralized power and the ability to defend itself. Israel's international reputation was further burnished under David's son Solomon. He undertook great building projects and set up international trading relationships. But the fall from this high point happened quickly. Solomon welcomed pagan influences and worshiped pagan deities.

Solomon's son Rehoboam was worse. He was a despot. First Kings 12 tells us that Rehoboam disregarded the counsel of his father's advisers and instead listened to his peers. They told him to say to the people, "My little finger is thicker than my father's loins. Now, whereas my father laid on you a heavy yoke, I will add to your yoke. My father disciplined you with whips, but I will discipline you with scorpions" (1 Kings 12:10-11). David's grandson took their advice, bragged about the size of this man-business, and things went terribly. The people stoned Rehoboam's minister in charge of forced labor and split the nation in two. Two southern tribes remained under the leadership of David's descendants and became known as Judah. The northern tribes placed themselves under the leadership of Jeroboam and kept the name Israel.

KINGS, PROPHETS, AND GOD'S PRESENCE

Jeroboam worried that his people would be seduced back into allegiance to Rehoboam if they continued their pilgrimages to the temple in Jerusalem, so he built local sacred sites. He had two calves made from gold and introduced them to the people as their gods. Not to be outdone, "Judah did what was evil in the sight of the LORD; they provoked him to jealousy with their sins that they committed, more than all that their ancestors had done" (1 Kings 14:22). They built sacred sites for pagan worship and began using prostitutes in their celebrations. The nation lost its spiritual and moral center; it succumbed to disunity and violence.

One of the voices speaking to the situation in the Northern Kingdom was the prophet Hosea. Israel didn't know who they were, didn't know the Law, and couldn't tell the story of their own unique existence. The rejection of shalom was so serious the land itself was affected. Here is Hosea speaking of how the land pays the price for Israel's identity crisis: "The LORD has an indictment against the inhabitants of the land. There is no faithfulness or loyalty, and no knowledge of God in the land. Swearing, lying, and murder, and stealing and adultery break out; bloodshed follows bloodshed. Therefore the land mourns, and all who live in it languish; together with the wild animals and the birds of the air, even the fish of the sea are perishing" (Hosea 4:1-3).

The depth of the divergence was symbolized by the fabulously corrupt king Ahab. In 1 Kings 16:30 we read that this Israelite king "did evil in the sight of the LORD more than all who were before him." This set the scene for the confrontation between Elijah and Ahab's pagan priests. The story has kept many a Sunday school kid from tipping into boredom. Elijah set up a barbecue contest, which he won in spectacular fashion. He killed the losers and then fled, afraid of the wrath of Ahab's wife. Elijah and his fellow prophets became characters not unlike Robin Hood and his band of merry men. They went in and out of hiding. They would pop up, annoy the corrupt officials, frustrate the common people, then take off again.

It's hard to find faithfulness to the covenant in the stories from these corrupt regimes. Yet the existence of the prophets themselves testifies that God had not left Judah and Israel to their shame. In this part of the Bible, God's opposition to evil is not some grand, end-of-story smackdown. It shows up in prophets' words and the chance for repentance they present. The role of the prophet was as important as that of the priest, the king, and the judge in the Hebrew Scriptures. The prophets had no actual institutional power, but their voices were important amid the division, rivalries, forgetfulness, and mixing of religious traditions we call **syncretism**.

Labeling prophets is something best done in hindsight. In the present there always seem to be too many voices. Opinions fly against each other. I remember going with some friends to the National Mall in Washington, D.C., to protest at a major public event. Our plans were mostly thwarted by congestion, long security lines, and the difficulty of finding a bathroom. We did eventually work our way through checkpoints and stood on the grass of the Mall. At our backs was a huge obelisk, and behind it the Lincoln Memorial. We were wannabe prophets.

Decades before, a true prophetic voice was broadcast from the steps of that memorial. It was that of Martin Luther King Jr., Baptist minister and leading figure in the civil rights movement. King was undoubtedly one of the most important preachers of the twentieth century. His sermons and speeches are some of the most significant pieces of rhetoric in American history. On the steps of the Lincoln Memorial, in August 1963, King was greeted with applause. Then he began: "I am happy to join with you today in what will go down in history as the greatest demonstration for freedom in the history of our nation." King moved slowly through the first several paragraphs of his speech, describing the situation of African Americans. He gathered energy as he proceeded. "Now is the time to make justice a reality for all of God's children," he said. King had to pause for applause with increasing frequency. "We will not be satisfied until justice rolls down like waters, and righteousness like a mighty stream," King said, quoting from the book of Amos. And then, his voiced laced with tension, King spoke about his dream, the American dream transformed: "I have a dream that one day on the red hills of Georgia, the sons of former slaves and the sons of former slave owners will be able to sit down together at the table of brother-hood." And on he went, pressing toward the end of his speech in marvelous cadence: "I have a dream that one day every valley shall be exalted, every hill and mountain shall be made low, the rough places will be made plain, and the crooked places will be made straight, and the glory of the Lord shall be revealed, and all flesh shall see it together." He was working with lines from Isaiah 40:4-5. Looking into the future when his dream would become a reality, King, with Abraham Lincoln looking over his shoulder, concluded with lines from a spiritual, "Free at last! Free at last! Thank God almighty, we are free at last!"[1]

The two biblical quotations within his speech were not random. King held a PhD in theology from Boston University. He wasn't just cherry-picking a few good lines; he was drawing on the power of the prophetic tradition. Both Amos and Isaiah were prophets. When we talk about "the prophets" in theological conversation, we might be referring to people with a specific role or to books of the Bible. There are the Major Prophets, which include the books of Isaiah, Jeremiah, Ezekiel, and Daniel, and the twelve Minor Prophets. The latter are sometimes simply referred to as the Book of the Twelve.[2] That's where we find the book of Amos, and the famous line from chapter 5 about justice rolling like water. The biblical prophets, much like King, spoke to a divided people that included both the oppressed and the oppressors. The prophets called for faithfulness to the covenant and stood against idolatry and injustice.

Both Israel and Judah were eventually overtaken by outside powers: first Israel in 722 BCE by the Assyrians, then Judah by the Babylonians. Jerusalem was destroyed in 586 BCE. The local inhabitants were carted off to foreign lands. Some of the prophets continued to minister to those who remained, and others did so in the centers of exile. One of the main questions they addressed was how God's priestly people could possibly continue their vocation in such a difficult situation. How could they be a blessed people when the land, the temple, and the whole sacrificial system were no longer a reality? It's here that we find the origins of the Judaism that Jesus and the disciples knew, which emphasized the synagogue, the biblical texts, the annual celebrations, and the traditions of the rabbis.

When Christians think about what hope looked like for these exiled people, we often miss that it was not merely inner or spiritual in nature. The prophets called for faithfulness to the covenant and the Torah, which gave shape to that faithfulness. The Torah, as we have seen, is practical and specific; it is a framework for justice. That is why preachers like Martin Luther King Jr. were right to make the connection between the prophets and their own quest for justice. The hope of the exiles and the call of the prophets give us a not-so-subtle hint that the salvation which God would bring is not merely inner and spiritual; it is as all-encompassing as shalom requires.

ESCHATOLOGY AND PROVIDENCE

The Baptist preacher on the steps of the Lincoln Memorial was not the first Christian to speak out about racial injustice. There were many before him. For some reason, God's prophetic inspiration seems to be coupled with divine patience. One of the earliest non-enslaved persons to speak against slavery in North America was a Quaker named John Woolman (1720–72). Quakers came to North America from England in search of a place where they could practice their faith free of England's theocratic coercion. By his mid-twenties, Woolman owned a business, and since he could read and write, he was sometimes hired to write wills. On one such assignment Woolman's conscience was pricked by a request that he include instructions for his client's slaves to be passed on to the client's children. The client was ill, which was why he wanted his will written up; nevertheless, Woolman refused to be complicit. In his journal, Woolman wrote, "I told the man that I believed the practice of continuing slavery . . . was not right, and that I had a scruple in my mind against doing writings of that kind . . . and I desired to be excused from going to write the will."[3]

Woolman's journals are filled with biblical references, and many are to the Hebrew prophets. Woolman eventually gave up his business altogether and made a living working as a tailor. He refused to wear dyed fabric because of the effects of the dyes on the workers who handled them. When traveling, he insisted on paying the slaves of his hosts. He refused to be served with silver, because he knew that enslaved people worked in deplorable conditions to produce the raw material. Woolman exemplified the prophetic tradition in word and in practice.

The prophetic books upon which King and Woolman drew span a period of significant change in the history of God's ambassador people. The great book of Isaiah appears to address audiences before their exile (chapters 1–39) and during it (chapters 40–66). Jeremiah ministered during the decline of Assyria and the rise of a successor empire, Babylon. Ezekiel, a priest who would have served in the temple, was instead called to minister to those forced to leave Jerusalem. The message of each of these prophets was set against the horizon of God's impending action.

When we're talking about what God will do, whether hopeful or fearful, we are talking about **eschatology**. Will tyrants and despots ever see justice? What, of all that we do, has lasting value? Will some of us be whisked off to heaven? These questions are eschatological questions. In the final chapter of the book of Daniel, we read this: "Many of those who sleep in the dust of the earth shall awake, some to everlasting life, and some to shame and everlasting contempt" (Daniel 12:2). This is one of the earliest, clearest statements in Scripture about a resurrection. Yet it's hard to know exactly what Daniel is describing. The book of Daniel is set in Babylon, but it comprises two distinct sections: the first contains the stories from the court in which Daniel served (chapters 1–6); the second is what we call an **apocalypse** (chapters 7–12). We commonly think of an apocalypse as the end of everything, but it's better to think of it as a great unveiling.

An apocalypse is where we see what's really going on, who's really in charge, and whose actions line up with the righteousness of God. There are two major sections of apocalyptic literature in the Bible. One is here in Daniel and the other is in the book of Revelation. Smaller chunks are in the Gospels as well. What makes this type of literature confusing for most modern readers is that it is all allegorical. Reading it is a bit like looking at a political cartoon where you need to know that one animal stands for a particular government or political party. Daniel's apocalyptic writing seems to be a coded description of God's judgment against Judah's leaders. Although it's hard to find consensus on how apocalyptic literature should be interpreted, most theologians agree that these parts of Scripture illustrate the just and loving character of God's governance.

One of the ideas that connects conversations about justice and conversations about eschatology is a concept called providence. Politicians in historically Christian countries often talk about "providence." They use it as a generic stand-in for God, or faith, or luck, or something like that. They want you to think that they believe whatever you do. In theological conversation, however, providence refers to God's anticipation of and control over events: from the color of your socks to the outcome of World War II. The notion of providence can be comforting and disconcerting in equal parts, but Christians believe in it. Christians believe that God is **omnipotent**, or all-powerful. The differences arise when we discuss what God's authority and power mean in relationship to history. A standard question here is whether God controls *everything* everything or lets some things work themselves out.

A warning light should be flashing on the page now. Here we're truly entering the territory of serious theology nerds. Actually, it's their territory and the territory of any of us who have ever wondered whether God has a specific plan for our lives or whether, say, the death of our cousin was orchestrated by the Creator of the universe. I must say at the outset that I think it's a bad idea to try to nail this stuff down completely. It isn't so much that we're trying to figure out how many angels can dance on the end of a pin; rather, we are trying to glue ice to a hot iron.

Christian thinkers like Martin Luther and many in the Reformed tradition—even Augustine in his later work—believed God determines the outcome of every event. We can refer to this as a belief in **meticulous providence**. In this view, the fact that you're reading this right now, in precisely your position and mindset, was determined by God in eternity past. Or to put it a bit differently: in this view, Abraham's faithful obedience, even his later willingness to sacrifice his son Isaac, was determined by God. Here the historical angle gets interesting. That's because it was from this Reformed camp that the most well-known dissident voice sprung, a fellow named Jacob Arminius (1560–1609). Arminius's parents died when he was a child; his mother was killed during the Spanish invasion of his Dutch hometown. Arminius was adopted by a pastor, received a good education, and went on to become a theology professor at the University of Leiden in Holland. That part of the world was known then, as it is now, for its freethinking and progressive culture. The view Arminius propounded from his academic post sometimes goes by his own name: Arminianism. More generically it is referred to as **limited providence**. This perspective, generally speaking at least, is supported by theologians working in the Orthodox tradition, along with most Anabaptists and those influenced by the work of John Wesley (1703–91).

I've written a bit about the historical distinction between the Orthodox and the Western church. The relationship is being rejiggered today, both at an official level and on the ground. The Orthodox are receiving new converts in the West, partly because of the lumberjack beards worn by their clergy, partly because of the community's clear historical connections to the early church, and partly because their priests can marry. I haven't yet said much about John Wesley, however. Wesley was an Anglican priest who, along with his brother, sparked a major church renewal movement on both sides of the Atlantic in the

middle of the eighteenth century. The Methodist tribe is one of
the results. What these folks have in common is the general view
that although the creator God could control every detail of our
lives, this isn't what God chooses to do. Instead, God allows the
sort of human freedom that means we could do things differently
than we do.

Let's focus, for a moment more, on the controversial figure of
Jacob Arminius. The divergence of opinion surrounding his views
became quite heated. Debates were held to sort things out, with
students, clergy, and politicians divided. Arminius died before
anything was settled. His followers, known as the Remonstrants,
continued to advocate his position. (I still hope that some former
student of mine will start a band with a name like Jane Doe and the
Remonstrants.) The more traditional Reformed view was clarified
some time later at the Synod of Dort. In English we summarize the
conclusions of this synod with the acronym TULIP: total depravity, unconditional election, limited atonement, irresistible grace,
and the perseverance of the saints. Each of these claims highlights
in some way the all-determining character of divine providence.

If you hang around with theology nuts long enough, someone
will ask you if you are a Calvinist or an Arminian. The question
is supposed to make you choose. I'm not convinced that you
have to. I think you can just say no. It's like someone asking you
whether it was the rain *or* the sun that made the lettuce grow.
Whenever we talk about the coming together of creation and
the Creator, human freedom and the freedom of God, we are
speaking about something that our language can't capture. We
don't need to think of the divine and the creaturely as mutually
exclusive causes. We don't need to say either God led you to a
new friend or social media did. These are things that appropri-
ately receive the label "mystery." They are mysterious not because
the Christian faith requires believing in the unbelievable. These
things are mysterious because our experience of creation doesn't

wholly prepare us to speak of how God works. This is why we should never feel that we must choose between praying for God's justice and working for it. Human action and the action of God are interwoven. It's not either one or the other.

Some of the exiles whom Jeremiah, Daniel, and the other prophets wrote about would eventually return. This story is chronicled in Ezra-Nehemiah, a book that is split in two in our Bibles but used to be one. The return was made possible when the Persians overthrew Babylon. Most likely, the Persians wanted the displaced people to see them as liberators. The opportunity did not entice everyone. The famous verse from Jeremiah—Jeremiah 29:11—that I referenced at the beginning of this book comes from this situation. The idea was that God had plans for those who *remained* in exile.

With the benefit of history, we can see what some of this might have meant. Up until the century before our own, some of the oldest living Jewish communities in the world were in territory that used to be part of the Persian Empire. In Jeremiah's day, Judaism became an exilic faith—one able to be at home in any part of the world. Jesus was a recipient of this tradition, and it undoubtedly played a role in the birthing of a new type of Judaism, one no longer marked by ethnic or geographic boundaries. This exilic and cosmopolitan version of Judaism is the precedent for global, multiethnic Christianity.

This blessing in exile, however, never seemed to fulfill the sort of thing that prophets like Joel and Amos anticipated when they wrote about "the day of the LORD." They anticipated a great reversal that would bring judgment and deliverance. At the beginning of the second chapter of Joel, we read, "Blow the trumpet in Zion; sound the alarm on my holy mountain! Let all the inhabitants of the land tremble, for the day of the LORD is coming, it is near—a day of darkness and gloom, a day of clouds and thick darkness!" (vv. 1-2). These verses echo the time when God gave the law to

Israel at Sinai—the darkness, the gloom, the earthquake. Joel was trying to tell his audience that the judgment of God penetrates all things, and that the future would connect with the past.

The words of Isaiah do something similar: "See, the former things have come to pass, and new things I now declare; before they spring forth, I tell you of them" (Isaiah 42:9). These eschatological texts point beyond themselves. "I am about to do a new thing," God says in Isaiah 43:19. The story isn't finished. However, the texts collected in the First Testament end, in the book of Malachi, with this: "Lo, I will send you the prophet Elijah before the great and terrible day of the LORD comes. He will turn the hearts of parents to their children and the hearts of children to their parents, so that I will not come and strike the land with a curse" (Malachi 4:5-6). Passages like these point to a renewed presence of God. They point to the revitalization of the priestly people. They point to the renewal of God's redemptive mission. This is where the Scriptures known by Jesus and his disciples come to an end. As with Martin Luther King's dream, there is a sense of anticipation, not completion. The work remains unfinished.

11

SHE WILL BEAR *a* SON

Incarnation

*It was their habit on a fixed day to assemble before daylight
and recite by turns a form of words to Christ as a god; and that
they bound themselves with an oath, not for crime, but not to
commit theft or robbery or adultery, not to break their word,
and not to deny a deposit when demanded. After this was done,
their custom was to depart, and to meet again to take food.*
—**Pliny (second century CE)**

The gospel of Mark begins with a look over the shoulder in
the direction from which we've just come. Where Malachi
pointed forward to a prophet who would precede the great and
terrible day of the LORD, the first chapter of Mark picks up with
a quotation from the prophet Isaiah: "See, I am sending my mes-
senger ahead of you, who will prepare your way, the voice of one

crying out in the wilderness: 'Prepare the way of the Lord, make his paths straight'" (Mark 1:2-3). The gospel writer's next words refer to John the baptizer and the next paragraph to the baptism of Jesus.

The links between these two parts of the Bible are indispensable: this is one story with one main, divine protagonist. Yet the distinctions are important too. The prophet Jeremiah looked forward to a new covenant. In 2 Corinthians, Paul speaks of this new covenant in the present tense: believers are, in his words, "ministers of a new covenant" (2 Corinthians 3:6). The words *covenant* and *testament* mean essentially the same thing in this context. It is this new covenant, or testament, that fully welcomes Gentiles (non-Jews). We can think of these two testaments as two floors in one building. They share a larger structure, and the second floor requires the first.

The two scriptural floors are close literarily and theologically. Historically, though, they are separated by several hundred years and several imperial changes. In the fourth century BCE, the Greeks, led by Alexander the Great, went to war with Persia. It was the Persians who had been in charge during the time of Malachi. Alexander conquered much of their territory. By the second century of the same era, the Jews in Judea had thrown off the yoke of Alexander's political descendants, who were known as the Seleucids. Under the powerful leadership of men like Judas the Maccabee, Jerusalem was reclaimed and temple practices restored. The machinery of the Hebrew monarchy, in the form of the Hasmonean dynasty, kicked into gear once again. It lasted roughly a century, until 63 BCE, when the Roman tidal wave swept across the Mediterranean basin.

In 37 BCE the Romans installed a regional king, Herod the Great. The Romans were builders: they established aqueducts, roads, racetracks, and so on. So was Herod. He launched an extraordinary construction campaign that shaped the built environment of Jesus' time. It included an immense new harbor on the Mediterranean, an expanded and remodeled temple in Jerusalem, and the now-famous desert fortress of Masada.

It was Herod who was in power when Jesus was born. It was he who Matthew tells us became infuriated when magi from the East, who were astrologers or wise men, failed to report the whereabouts of this new king. It was he who Matthew says "sent and killed all the children in and around Bethlehem who were two years old or under" (Matthew 2:16). For Matthew, the fulfillment of the words of Jeremiah was obvious: "A voice was heard in Ramah, wailing and loud lamentation, Rachel weeping for her children; she refused to be consoled, because they are no more" (v. 18).

In theological conversation we speak of Mary's unexpected pregnancy and the birth of Jesus as the **incarnation**. It's God's taking on flesh. The incarnation is the heart of the good news. But in history it was accompanied by deep tragedy—the blood of children and the wailing of mothers. As I write this chapter, news breaks of yet another mass shooting in our own century. A young man armed with high-powered weapons burst into a church and opened fire, dealing death in an attempt to prove a vicious point, to make a statement, to work out his own issues. Surely Herod's world and ours are not as different as the intervening millennia could make us think.

INCARNATE IN SUFFERING

One sometimes wonders if it's a good idea to bring children into such a world. Why bring the vulnerable into a time and place that will take advantage of them? Why bring babies into a time and place that will break their flesh to prove a point? Yet it is into this world that a young Jewish woman brought a male child. Some ancient Christian communities would refer to her as "the bearer of God." Yet Mary and her husband were forced to uproot and flee with their child to Egypt. This, Matthew tells his readers, was to fulfill the words of the prophet Hosea: "Out of Egypt I have called my son" (Matthew 2:15).

Like the kings, priests, prophets, and judges of old, this child would stand before God on behalf of all of Israel. In doing that for the priestly people, he would do so for the world—one son in flesh for a son in spirit. This is big, grandiose stuff, bigger than the Olympics, bigger than the stock market. The work of God here is so epic that John, writer of the latest of the Gospels, takes up philosophical language to describe the meaning of this birth: "In the beginning was the Word, and the Word was with God, and the Word was God" (John 1:1). But this birth was, historically speaking at least, a small-town affair greeted by nobody more pompous than herders of sheep. Such is the height of the biblical drama.

The concept of the Word (*logos* in Greek) seems to us a poetic flourish. However, it was familiar to John's original readers. Five hundred years or so earlier, the Greek philosopher Heraclitus used the term to speak of the rational structure that undergirded the world. For Aristotle, a century after Heraclitus, the term applied to the logical aspect of an argument. For the Stoics, yet another hundred years closer to the birth of Christ, the *logos* was more like a living thing. It was the active agent of reason that made the universe tick. This, then, is what the gospel writer brings to mind for his readers: this Logos was in the beginning with God and was God.

John changes things. We expect the ball to travel straight, but it hooks. John invokes a personal pronoun: "*He* was in the beginning with God" (John 1:2, emphasis added). And a few verses later: "And the Word became flesh and lived among us, and we have seen his glory, the glory as of a father's only son, full of grace and truth" (v. 14). The code that animates the universe takes on skin and is birthed into the world through the effort of a new Abraham, a woman named Mary. Her son would study Torah, become a teacher in his own right, and suffer a criminal's execution.

I mentioned earlier that my theological studies took me from Virginia to Toronto, Ontario. Toronto is an immensely diverse city, and studying there brought me into contact with Christians from around the world. Each was, in one way or another, affected by Mary's boy. I lived in a residence hosted by a theological college in the center of the city. When there were big protests at the provincial capital, I could hear them. Pastors, priests, and church leaders from around the world studied and lectured nearby. These living and breathing witnesses to the global theological conversation prompted me to read more widely than I had before. Going back to the library once more, I found the work of the Japanese theologian Kazoh Kitamori.

Kitamori is probably one of the few people in the world whose life was substantially changed by reading a theology essay. As a high school student, Kitamori read a paper about Martin Luther that echoed his own search for God. He was so affected by the work that he decided to go to the Lutheran seminary in Tokyo. Kitamori went on to become a prolific theologian, writing more than forty books and pastoring a congregation for more than forty years. Of the many books Kitamori wrote, his most famous in the English-speaking world is *Theology of the Pain of God*.[1]

Talking about the incarnation puts us in the territory of divine pain. Nevertheless, it was a passage from Jeremiah 31 that prompted Kitamori to write his celebrated book. In that passage, God comforts the exiles by promising that they would go home one day. Here is the key passage, verses 18-20: "Indeed I heard Ephraim pleading. . . . Is Ephraim my dear son? Is he the child I delight in?" And now the crucial sentence: "Therefore I am deeply moved for him; I will surely have mercy on him."

What stood out to Kitamori was the phrase "I am deeply moved," or as it was rendered in the Japanese Literary Version, "my heart is pained." As you might have guessed, it's the word *pained* that was significant to Kitamori. Luther had rendered the phrase "my heart is broken." The King James Version says, "my bowels are troubled." Kitamori was struck by the connection between pain and mercy. From this initial insight he noticed other parts of Scripture expressing something similar. Hebrews 2:10 was one such passage: "It was fitting that God . . . should make the pioneer of their salvation perfect through sufferings." There it sounds as if God suffered in Jesus. Reflecting on this passage, Kitamori writes, "The pain of God is part of his essence! . . . The Bible reveals that the pain of God belongs to his *eternal being*."[2]

Western theology has been reluctant to speak of God as being affected by anything, at least on a deep ontological level. Which is to say on the level of God's being. That's why God is traditionally described as **impassible**. That word comes from the Latin *passibilis*, which implies an ability to suffer or experience emotion. *Im*passibility, then, is the quality that allows God *not* to be affected by pain or pleasure from the actions of another. Impassibility is usually described as a consequence of God's **aseity**: the idea that since God is absolutely independent from creation, creation cannot affect God.

For some of us, this will sound obvious. We think, Of course God can't be pushed around. For others, impassibility and aseity make it sound as if God is willfully out of touch—like some irritable, self-obsessed grandpa in the sky. It might be counterintuitive, but these attributes are intended to help us avoid *both* of these ways of thinking about God. Part of the reason for emphasizing impassibility, in Western theology at least, is to make it clear that God is not capricious. We don't have to approach God while cowering in fear of an unpredictable grouch. We can depend on God's love because God doesn't change. God isn't affected by a lunch that didn't sit well or by disrespectful neighbors.

What was important for Kitamori, though, was the connection between our experience of God's mercy and God's experience of pain. It is in this connection that we understand God's love, and it is in this connection that we can begin to actually speak of God's essence. As Kitamori says in his conclusion, "The inner heart of God is pain."[3] Kitamori was reacting to a theological tradition that he believed was influenced by an underlying Greek philosophy to such an extent that it obscured the witness of Scripture. Even Martin Luther's theology of the cross, which Kitamori admired, did not fully capture the way God was affected by the suffering of creatures. Luther famously followed Paul in resolving to know nothing "except Jesus Christ, and him crucified" (1 Corinthians 2:2). It was Luther's way of turning from the grand confidence of medieval theological systems to a humble reliance of Scripture. Yet Kitamori believed that the inability of Western theology to appreciate the pain of God got in the way of hearing the biblical message. The concept of divine suffering provided an important link between Japanese culture and the biblical world.

As you might expect, and as I learned in my academic seminars, ideas like this have had a mixed reception. Although Kitamori's insight stemmed from one of the prophets, the larger debate centers on the incarnation. It seems obvious that Jesus suffered, a fact that has been a source of encouragement for millions. We affirm that in identifying with human creatures, God knows and understands what it is like for us to suffer, even to die. But did God actually suffer on the cross? Did God—creator and sustainer of the universe—die? Questions like these drove the ancient church to clarify how we speak about the relationship of divinity and humanity in Jesus.

REJIGGERING THE FAMILY TREE

We can't talk about the incarnation without discussing one of the main ways ancient Christians understood its impact. The key voice here is that of Irenaeus (130–202). Depending on whom you ask, and depending on what they mean, many historians identify this guy as the first "real" theologian. Whatever that might imply about others, we do know that Irenaeus was a second-century bishop in what is now Lyon, France. Irenaeus was born into a Christian family, which wasn't common in the early days of the church. There weren't that many Christian families to be born into. Another important part of his biography is that Irenaeus heard Polycarp (69–156) preach. Polycarp, in turn, was believed to have been an apprentice of the gospel writer John. Jesus to John to Polycarp to Irenaeus. Compared to almost everyone else who has jumped into the theological conversation, Irenaeus wasn't far removed from the source! This connection is important, because the witness of people like Polycarp and Irenaeus makes it unlikely that the ancient stewards of the redemption story could have just made up stuff about Jesus.

In the history of theology, Irenaeus is best known for describing what Jesus accomplished as **recapitulation**. The root is the Greek word *capix*, which means "head." Jesus stands in Adam's place as the new head of humanity. Just as the head of a stream can affect everything below it, so Jesus determines the character of those who follow him. He replaces Adam as the head of the river of humanity. Changing the metaphor slightly, we can say that just as all of humanity was once judged under Adam's sin, and just as all of Israel was judged through the deeds of a king, so now Jesus becomes our legal representative. The Greek word that stands behind much of this thinking is *anakephalaiosis*, found in Romans 13. It's usually translated as "summed up" or "condensed." In Romans 13, it is used to describe the way love sums up the law. For ancient theologians like Irenaeus, this is what Jesus does as the new head of humanity: we are all pulled together and freed through the work of this one human creature.

This draws our attention to the importance of the incarnation itself—that is, the importance of the fact that God took on human flesh. In our rush to unpack the meaning of the cross or the resurrection, we sometimes overlook the incarnation. In Romans,

Paul identifies himself as a servant of Jesus Christ, "who was descended from David according to the flesh and was declared to be Son of God with power according to the spirit of holiness by resurrection from the dead, Jesus Christ our Lord" (Romans 1:3-4). For Paul, Jesus' death and resurrection do not slip from view but are of one piece with his fleshly connection to David and his identity as the Son of God. The words of the gospel of John are apt too: "And the Word became flesh and lived among us, and we have seen his glory, the glory as of a father's only son, full of grace and truth" (John 1:14). Although it isn't clear that Jesus or his disciples immediately grasped things quite this way, it wouldn't take long before Christians would speak of Jesus as the very presence of God in human flesh.

One of the reasons the incarnation became so significant in Irenaeus's theology is that he needed to counter **gnosticism**. Gnostic views have been a constant antagonist to the Christian faith. At its core, a gnostic perspective—and there are many variations—believes that flesh and the rest of material reality are evil. These views still exist today in the form of Christians who believe sex is inherently evil or who think that Christians hope to live as disembodied spirits.

MORE THAN WORDS

Late one night a little while before I moved to Toronto, I found myself thumping the end of a broom handle on the ceiling above my bed. I was renting a basement apartment from an older couple. It's normal enough for couples to argue, and for neighbors to overhear them. But this house had no sound-deadening insulation, and my landlords were losing their hearing. I had gotten used to the loud TV and overhearing one-half of their phone conversations, but the arguments were another matter. I could not bring myself to ask about the arguments. I could only thump periodically on the ceiling. The couple had been pleasant at first.

Now I knew—and they knew I knew—that their affable self-presentation wasn't everything.

The frustrating living situation coincided with what, for other reasons, turned out to be a lonely spring. I contemplated the liturgical season of Lent in a way I never had before. In fact, never before had it occurred to me that the spiritual exercise of Lent might be valuable. Staring into the darkness as Lent ticked by, listening to an elderly couple yell at each other, knowing that the next time I saw them we would smile at each other like actors in a neighborhood commercial: well, it made me wonder what the death of a first-century Jewish rabbi could possibly mean to us. What did it matter to a bitter couple with most of their life behind them? What did it matter to me, a lonely graduate student? The answers I had been given—"Jesus came to die for our sins"—didn't seem so much wrong as narrow and abstract.

The life of Jesus, and its impact on humans, must surely be more than a theory. If it doesn't change—objectively change—how we relate to God, to each other, and even to ourselves, then there is nothing more to the Christian faith than the theological conversation. Throughout this book I've been trying to make the case that theology is integral to the Christian faith. My point here is that theology is a second-order activity. The real stuff of the Christian life is changed lives, new hope, and a deeper knowledge of God. We don't really get Christian theology without grasping that. And if there is no *that*—if there is nothing here for an older couple needing to be pulled back into vibrant relationship with each other or for a young student needing community—then, well, Christian faith is not what it claims to be. All this must be more than theory if John's description of the incarnation is true and if the early church was right to believe that being in Christ meant they were a new kind of people.

There are lots of ways to talk about the effectiveness of Jesus' life, death, and resurrection. We can say Jesus paid a debt. We can say he rescued or saved us. We can say he defeated the powers of evil. We can say he welcomed us into God's family. We can say he gives humanity a new head. All these are metaphors, and all these are biblical. The Anglican theologian Scot McKnight suggests that a basic movement holds all these possible descriptions together: "identification for incorporation."[4] That is, in Jesus, God identifies with human creatures and incorporates us into his victory over death. This liberates us from the powers of evil that hold us captive. McKnight is drawing on Hebrews 2:14-15: "Since, therefore, the children share flesh and blood, he himself likewise shared the same things, so that through death he might destroy the one who has the power of death, that is, the devil, and free those who all their lives were held in slavery by the fear of death." Like any priest, Jesus identifies with us and with God. In so doing, Jesus can make atonement for the sin that disrupts the well-being of creation. To be in Christ, to be a Christian, is to be one who has put off the old way of things like a worn-out shirt and put on Christ, a new way of being human, a way characterized by love.

Dietrich Bonhoeffer once observed that the complex interrelationships of Scripture can make reading it feel overwhelming. The feeling of being overwhelmed, though, is appropriate because, as Paul says in Colossians 2:3, "all the treasures of wisdom and knowledge" are hidden in Christ.[5] That's what Bonhoeffer believed. To speak of the atoning work of Jesus, then, is to speak of something like a whirlpool at the center of Scripture. We enter Scripture through Christ's work and the Spirit's power. As we cycle back around, we find that Scripture points us to what God has done in Christ. Exploring theology is little more than discovering the implications of this basic conviction. This basic conviction draws in the full breadth of Scripture and the full breadth of our lives.

12

YOU SHALL CALL
HIS NAME JESUS

Reconciliation

*Kingdom action takes place in the world in the middle of the
societal ballpark. But it's a different game.*
   —Donald B. Kraybill

We were sitting in a stone meeting room down the street
from the Church of the Nativity in Bethlehem. Our host
was a Palestinian pastor. He and his church were caught between
the territorial ambitions of a neighboring state and an urge to
violent resistance bubbling up in surrounding neighborhoods. We
listened to the pastor tell us what it was like to not be allowed to
move about freely. We heard about having years of work reduced
to ruins. We heard about feeling invisible. Churches in this part

of the world are some of the oldest anywhere, but many outsiders still don't think there is such a thing as a Palestinian Christian.

I have traveled to Israel and Palestine twice. As much as I wanted to walk in the places where the biblical characters had walked, I also wanted to hear from people like this pastor. I wanted to get a feel for the land, to stroll through an olive grove and look out over the Sea of Galilee. I also wanted to know what it was like to be a Christian there. I wondered what it was like to preach about Jesus at the confluence of three faith traditions, a place where tension was thick and where history lay close to the surface. I asked the pastor how he could sustain his ministry amid the tension and roadblocks.

The man was well educated, with a PhD from a European university and a command of several languages. It seemed to me that he could have found work anywhere. In response to my question, he admitted that sometimes he wanted to quit. Nevertheless, the people of Bethlehem were his people and the ancient city was his home. As for what he did when his community's projects were deliberately damaged? He said that he just started more projects. In addition to being a pastor, he had helped found a college, a guest house, an international center, a model school, a media center, an art gallery, a conference center, a restaurant, a health center . . . and he had written some sixteen books. I couldn't help but wonder what would happen if people saw more examples of pastoral ministry like this—politically engaged, significant, daring. Would more young people take such a calling seriously?

Later, as I walked the city's streets and ventured into the countryside, I was struck at one moment by how things seemed so totally different from the days of Jesus . . . and then moments later I found myself almost expecting the Jewish rabbi to amble over the hill with his disciples. There is a temptation in the spiritual life to forget Jesus' context, to make him into a timeless hologram hovering somewhere around the time of our grandparents. We are forgetful, not just of Jesus' social or political context, but also of the way his story is situated in the literary context of Scripture. Luke 24 is one example. Jesus has just shared a meal with his disciples when we read this:

> He said to them, "These are my words that I spoke to you while I was still with you—that everything written about me in the law of Moses, the prophets, and the psalms must be fulfilled." Then he opened their minds to understand the scriptures, and he said to them, "Thus it is written, that the Messiah is to suffer and to rise from the dead on the third day, and that repentance and forgiveness of sins is to be proclaimed in his name to all nations, beginning from Jerusalem." (vv. 44-47)

"Everything written about me"—that's important, because few, if any, of those who wrote the Hebrew Scriptures had any notion that what they were writing pointed toward a life like that of Jesus. Yet here Jesus indicates that he fulfills the calling of Israel and reshapes several central aspects of being God's people: His body fulfills the purpose of the temple. His servanthood refashions the role of the king. The mandate he gives his disciples expands the concept of promised land to the whole of creation. And yes, Gentiles join Jews as spiritual inheritors of Abraham. There's more to the context of Jesus than the buildings and hills outlined in our coloring books.

FOUR ROLES

One way to describe the meaning of Jesus is to think of his ministry in relationship to some of the key roles in ancient Israel: prophet, priest, king, and judge. These roles aren't always clearly distinguishable, but they can help us speak of the multiple facets of Jesus' work. The prophets called ancient Israel back to their Scriptures and back to the implications of their covenant relationship with God. They challenged the usual way of things. They reinterpreted and reapplied the great stories and laws in new contexts. In our contemporary context, some Palestinian theologians have had to play this role for Western Christians. These contemporary prophets point again to Scripture to disrupt our easy conclusions. Prophets show that the old words still have bite.

Jesus was just such a person. He reinterpreted Scripture as a prophet and as a rabbinic teacher within the first-century world. There are many examples of this, but one we shouldn't miss comes from the book of Matthew. Matthew tells the story of Jesus through five blocks of teaching set off by key stories. The example I'm thinking of comes from the first block of teaching, chapters 5–7. The section begins with a simple phrase: "When Jesus saw the crowds, he went up the mountain" (Matthew 5:1). This "mountain" probably took no more than twenty minutes to climb, so calling it a "mountain" wasn't intended to show off Jesus' stamina. It was intended to remind readers of the time that Moses received God's law on a mountain. Jesus is presenting a new law. It isn't just what he says that's important; it's the staging.

Jesus begins to teach: "Blessed are the . . ." Even that phrase has contextual significance. His Jewish audience would have noticed the parallel to bits of their Scriptures. They might have thought of Psalm 1, which begins the same way. Jesus immerses himself in the biblical thought world and revises it. His first line on the mountain concludes with "poor in spirit, for theirs is the kingdom of heaven" (Matthew 5:3). Each of the five major blocks of teaching in Matthew center on the kingdom theme. Jesus is outlining the way of life for his followers. Later he says, "Blessed are the peacemakers, for they will be called children of God. Blessed are those who are persecuted for righteousness' sake, for theirs is the kingdom of heaven" (Matthew 5:9-10). This is the sort of life to be lived by God's example people.

When we say that Jesus presents a new way of life—you could call it a new national constitution—we shouldn't think he is in absolute opposition to the old version. In verse 17 of the same chapter Jesus says, "Do not think that I have come to abolish the law or the prophets; I have come not to abolish but to fulfill." Where the old law forbade murder, Jesus instructs his followers to guard against the spirit of murder. He tells them, too, to be proactive in settling disputes. The Torah forbade sex with someone you weren't married to, but in the kingdom, Jesus says, citizens avoid thinking of the bodies of others in possessive or objectifying ways. The old law had careful provisions for taking oaths, but Jesus says citizens of the new kingdom should always speak reliably and carefully. Why swear on a stack of Bibles unless you don't usually tell the truth? Kingdom citizens shouldn't retaliate; they should love their enemies. Like the Law of Moses, the intention of Jesus' law is to show how to live rightly with God's creatures in God's world. Unlike that law, this way of life turned attention away from boundary behaviors and toward wholly renewed lives.

The followers of Jesus, just like those of Moses, were welcomed into a community marked by God's gift of moral guidance. The intent isn't dutiful drudgery, but well-nourished, satisfying lives. And Jesus lived this as much as he taught it. The block of teaching in Matthew 5–7 is followed by stories of Jesus healing a leprous man and a centurion's servant. Those with leprosy and those who were servants were not central characters in first-century Jewish life, but Jesus includes them. Jesus fulfills both the calling of humanity and the "calling" of God. That is, he does what humans were created to do *and* what God had covenanted to do. Centuries later Irenaeus said that "the Son of God became the Son of Man" so that we might all be adopted as children of God. Jesus was a prophet and a teacher, yes. Yet his words and way of life matter for Christians because we think he was much more than that.

WAYPOINTS ON THE TRAIL OF CHRISTOLOGY

In English translations of the First Testament, one of the names used for God is "LORD of hosts," or "God Almighty." When these same texts were translated into Greek centuries before the time of Jesus, the term used was *Pantocrator*. Some New Testament writers, most notably John of Patmos, used the term. John uses it nine times in the book of Revelation. Ancient Christians used the term as a title for an icon depicting Jesus. The oldest one still in existence was found in a monastery in the Sinai Desert. It was created in the sixth or seventh century.

The *Pantocrator* icon itself is pretty simple: it depicts Jesus from the shoulders up, looking ahead with a book in his left hand. His right hand, with two fingers slightly raised, is held in front of his sternum. If you look closely at this icon, you'll notice that it isn't intended to be a photorealistic presentation of Jesus. You'll notice that Jesus' face looks like two faces cut and pasted together. The left and right halves don't match. The skin tone is different, the expressions aren't identical, and the eyes look in different directions. This isn't an accident; the icon is a powerful bit of theological writing. In bearing the title *Pantocrator*, this icon identifies Jesus with the creator God. In dividing Jesus' face in two, the artist depicts a long-held claim that Jesus is truly human and truly divine.

Up to this point we've been speaking about Jesus in terms of the biblical story line. I've been outlining what we sometimes call **narrative Christology**. We haven't been focusing as much on *what* Jesus is as on what he does and how he fits into the story of ancient Israel. This probably hasn't seemed particularly strange. It fits with the general drift of the Gospels, where Jesus' biography is presented and where he is woven into the tapestry of the Hebrew Bible. Narrative Christology is all about the story.

The notion that Jesus does what God committed to do suggests other descriptions. We see these crop up throughout the New Testament. One particularly important example is found in the second chapter of Philippians. There Paul writes, "Let the same mind be in you that was in Christ Jesus, who, though he was in the form of God, did not regard equality with God as something to be exploited" (vv. 5-6). If you look that passage up in your Bible, you'll probably notice a shift in the way the text is laid out after the first comma. It appears that right there Paul quotes an ancient hymn. Like the Gospels, this ancient hymn tells a story. Unlike the Gospels, it grapples with the need for other ways to describe Jesus. So it speaks of Jesus being in the form of God and being equal with God. As brief as it is, this passage is evidence that early Christians were exploring descriptions of Jesus and his reconciling work that had profound ontological elements. That is, they were trying to put together the fact that he had a specific human genealogy, as we read in Matthew 1, with the lofty connections to God made in passages like John 1, Hebrews 1, and Colossians 1. In Colossians 1, for instance, Jesus is described as "the image of the invisible God" in whom "all things hold together" (vv. 15, 17). That is lofty stuff for the son of . . . well, anyone.

These biblical examples show that the use of ontological descriptions for Jesus' significance runs back just about to the beginning of the Christian community. Nevertheless, it was the fourth century that saw the development of the language many of us use to describe Jesus. A landmark meeting called the Council of Nicaea took place during that time. Nicaea isn't a person's name; it's the name of the town where the emperor Constantine briefly lived. We call the event that took place there a council because church leaders from across the empire took part. Today we would probably call it a convention or a conference.

The story of the Nicene Council begins in a city farther south named Alexandria. Alexandria was an intellectual center in the ancient world; it lies on the southern edge of the Mediterranean, near the mouth of the Nile River. The drama began with a disagreement between the local bishop named Alexander (d. 326) and a pastor named Arius (250–336). The two men didn't think of Jesus in the same way.

Arius understood the Logos to be a creature, a uniquely important creature, but one who by definition did not fully share the Father's status or eternality. Part of the reason Arius and others held this view so strongly was because they believed it was a necessary way to defend God's **apatheia**. Apatheia is linked to some of the other divine attributes we've discussed, like aseity and impassibility. Apatheia means that God cannot suffer or be passive. The point wasn't to question the reality of divine love, but to reject the view that God's being could be affected by anything in creation. God's perfection, it was believed, demanded a static, unchanging existence. For Arius, this meant that the incarnation and suffering of Christ could not, properly speaking, have happened to God. He believed these things happened to the created Logos.

Arius's views were not particularly radical in Alexandria. They actually fit quite nicely with the dominant intellectual currents there. However, they didn't sit well with the bishop, Alexander, who thought Arius didn't identify Jesus closely enough with the Creator. Arius returned the favor by claiming Alexander's view was a form of **modalism**. Modalism is the idea that the Father, Son, and Spirit are different modes of God's self-presentation. God can appear as the Father at one point, as the Son at another, or off to the side somewhere as the Spirit. God, in the modalist perspective, is just never these at the same time.

Christians in Alexandria chose sides; people shouted and pushed each other in the streets. There were riots. Alexander, in his role as bishop, called a local council, which agreed that Arius was wrong and suggested that he lose his job. Alexander took the council's advice and sacked Arius. The conflict spread so widely that it worried the emperor. He thought the theological difference might compromise the unity of his empire. He stepped in and called for a conference at Nicaea in 325. Over three hundred church leaders attended. The council rejected the position of Arius. They invoked an extrabiblical term, **homoousios**, to clarify how they thought Scripture should be read. The term *homoousios* means that two things are of the same substance. The council said this was true of the Incarnate Word and God the Father. The council also affirmed that Christ was not created but "begotten." That was supposed to mean that the life and ministry of Jesus had its origin in the eternal God and to rule out the idea that the Logos was created in time. They did not think that this implied that God suffered; they didn't want to compromise on divine apatheia. The ancients seemed to see only two alternatives: either God was compelled to suffer or God did not suffer at all. More recent theological developments have stressed that God freely chose to suffer in Christ. God didn't have to, but freely did so out of love.

Let's give the ancient world our attention for just a little while longer. This is an important part of the theological conversation. Even though the emperor had hosted the Nicene Council, his will to enforce it gradually evaporated. In fact, Constantine became sympathetic to Arianism, and Arius himself was brought back into fellowship. Meanwhile, Bishop Alexander died. He was succeeded by a fellow who would become quite famous, a man named Athanasius (296–373) who was nicknamed the Black Dwarf. One of Athanasius's most famous works is *On the Incarnation of the Word*. In it the North African bishop argues for the equality of substance in both God the Son and God the Father. His opposition to Arianism earned him a forced exile in Germany, courtesy of the emperor.

The issue had to be taken up again by church leaders in 381, this time in Constantinople proper. A key development in the intervening years was one pushed by Athanasius and the Cappadocians. Where *homoousios* named the commonality between Father, Son, and Spirit, the Cappadocians argued that the term *hypostasis* should be used to name the distinction between the three. *Hypostasis* is usually translated into English as "person." Therefore we speak of the triune God as sharing one substance and comprising three persons.

Part of person-ness is being in relationship. Think about how someone might describe you by listing your relationships: you're the child of someone, the friend of someone else, or a student of whomever. Similarly, under the tutelage of the Cappadocians, we see that we can't talk about the identity of the first person of the Trinity without saying that this person is the source of the Son and the Spirit. The Son's identity can't be described without saying that he bears the image of the Father. The Spirit's identity can't be described without saying that the Spirit is the flow of the Father's wisdom and life-giving power to us. We speak of these as three, eternally in relationship, but they are one. We can't name one member of the Trinity without implicitly naming the others. Not only is each in relationship with the others, but the life of each flows into and out of the others. The Cappadocians described this as **perichoresis**: the presence of each member of the Trinity in the other. This is a feature of the life of the triune God but, by analogy, is also a feature of human relationships.

The council at Constantinople reaffirmed the basic logic of Nicaea and said more about the Holy Spirit, affirming the Third Person as equally divine. The resulting document is known as the Nicene Creed. It could technically be called the Niceno-Constantinopolitan Creed, but who wants to say all that? The Nicene Creed is used in worship services the world over as a summary of the core beliefs of the Christian faith. The creed itself begins with the phrase "We believe in . . ." and is made up of three short paragraphs, or articles, on each member of the Trinity. The creed does not contain everything that is important to the faith. Little is said, for instance, about the content of Jesus' teaching. It doesn't say much about Jesus' life at all. Even so, a lot is jammed into this little document. There is even an important description of the church and a bit about baptism, forgiveness, and the world to come—all packed into the article on the Holy Spirit.

I haven't always had the highest appreciation for the Nicene Creed. There was a time in my studies when I was convinced that its links to imperial concerns irrevocably distorted the message of Jesus. That has the makings of a good conspiracy theory. However, now that I've been teaching and pastoring, I've come to find the Nicene Creed helpful in two key ways. First, it is simply a useful summary of the faith. I often talk to people who have so many questions about their faith and are so unsure of how to sort the center from the edges that they would like nothing better than a historically grounded summary. The Nicene Creed is exactly that. The creed can also serve as a short grammar guide. If you've ever studied a foreign language and been allowed to take a little note card into a translation exam, you know what I mean. We don't need to feel limited to the specifics of the words of the Nicene Creed, yet the creed helps us know how to talk about God. We should affirm and deny the same types of things the creed does. Wherever I've traveled, I've always felt a sense of commonality when I learn that Christians there too affirm not just the Bible but also this grammar guide.

THE TRINITY IN THE MODERN AGE

Not long after I listened to the pastor from Palestine, I came across the work of a contemporary Spanish theologian named Antonio González. González, an Anabaptist theologian, spent years in Latin America. For him, trinitarian doctrine coheres with the struggle of those who suffer because it "derives from the concrete Christian experience of liberation in the present."[1] What he means is that this trinitarian way of describing God is not only a way of making sense of the Bible or the development of Christian thought; it is also deeply connected to the experience of the Spirit in the grit of life. To speak of God as triune is to speak about

God's profound solidarity with human creatures. This is not just a theoretical solidarity but one that comes to the fore in the story of Jesus' forsakenness on the cross. González says that in Jesus, God personally experiences "the fate of those who appear to be abandoned by God in history." In that moment, God, who is called upon, does not come. "Christ is not saved from the cross," González says. Yet "this experience of abandonment . . . is not a rupture in the divinity, for on the cross it is the one and only God who personally suffers the fate of Christ."[2]

The lonely death of Jesus is not just an event in the story of Jesus. It is a trinitarian event. Jesus lives and dies as God's solidarity with human creatures. Two thousand years later, the Spirit makes this solidarity real to us. That we encounter the stuff of God in Christ is reason to pay attention to the life and the teachings of Jesus. It's reason to take Jesus' Sermon on the Mount seriously—whether we're on a hill in ancient Judea, in Africa's Great Rift Valley, on the vast prairies of North America, or on some side street in one of our world's ever-growing cities.

13

HE SHALL SAVE HIS PEOPLE *from* THEIR SINS

Atonement

It is no great feat to love the lovable . . . but to love the unlovable, to love those who do not love us, to love our enemies—that is love. That is impossible . . .
—**John Caputo**

You could write a few words on a card, drop it on the floor of the library, and walk away. Nothing would happen. Nothing, that is, unless someone picked up your note. And still nothing unless they could make some sense of what you wrote. And whatever sense they might make would be determined not just by your words, but by the larger context: what the reader may know about you, or maybe what was in the news that day. If you are working out in a gym and someone overhears you tell a friend that you want "big guns," they will probably assume you are talking about your biceps. If you talk about big guns when you are in a school and looking at a bad grade you received on a paper, the hearer might worry that you have other things in mind. Words are powerful, but they don't work alone.

In one of his letters to Timothy, Paul says that Scripture, this collection of words, is useful for teaching and training. These words can help us lead lives of worth and meaning. If you spend enough time with Christians, you'll notice that some of us refer to Scripture as "the word of God." It's a way of saying that even though the Bible is shaped by the assumptions and experiences of its authors, it is also something God uses to communicate to us. The biblical writers generally use the term "word of God" to refer to God's speech, through a prophet maybe, and they refer to the Bible itself as "Scripture." In the famous beginning of the gospel of John, for instance, the line "in the beginning was the Word" does not refer to the Bible. It refers to Jesus. In writing we can make a distinction between the *Word* of God, referring to Jesus, and the *word* of God, referring to other forms of God's speech. The primary task of the word of God (Scripture) is to witness to the Word of God—Jesus the Anointed One. There are words, words, words, and then the Word.

If the entire contemporary theological conversation—words about the Word—were taking place in one cafeteria and people joined tables according to their interests, one of the most popular tables would be the one where people were talking about the atonement. Folks at that table would be talking about the suffering and death of Jesus and trying to figure out how it worked and why it mattered. More specifically, they would be debating whether God used violence to fix things. There is a lot of conversation about this right now, partly because we've become more conscious of the way our theological speech can encourage violence.

If the atonement hasn't come up in your own conversations, you might not immediately see the problem. The issue for many is that if God deliberately did violence to Jesus in the crucifixion, or if God somehow requires violence to restore shalom, doesn't this make God a divine child abuser? Or, to put it another way: Doesn't the cross mean that at the heart of things it is violence that does the heavy lifting? How does this fit with Jesus' command to love our enemies, or his claim that following him requires us to take up our cross?

Or think of the core of New Testament ethics—love for God and love for our neighbor. How does a violent, Jesus-killing God fit with that? This question isn't limited to the rarefied air of advanced theological studies. People talk about it in churches after a service, and worship teams discuss it when they choose music.

Some of the most provocative recent work on this topic has been written by a Mennonite theologian named J. Denny Weaver. (Weaver is the only theologian I've heard of who has had a university mascot named after him. The school where he spent most of his career is led into sporting glory by a furry J. Denny *Beaver*.) In his book *The Nonviolent Atonement*, Weaver suggests that modern Christian thinkers have been so captivated by the way the criminal justice system links crime and punishment that they talk about the atonement in the same way. The problem he sees—or one of them at least—is that the predominant view of atonement normalizes violence. One could imagine, for instance, that people in positions of privilege could point to the violence of the atonement as a rationale for why they treat others so poorly. Weaver finds insight in the wisdom of Black, feminist, and other theologies. "By being aware of and articulating their own contexts," he writes, "black and feminist and womanist theologies shone a bright light on the fact that the received theology of

Christendom in general and in satisfaction atonement in particular also have a context."[1] With that in mind, Weaver has tried to revisit Scripture without the assumption that Jesus' death satisfies an abstract legal requirement.

THE PROBLEM HAS MANY FACES

If we are just joining this conversation, a simple question might be the best way to move forward. A question like this: What is the problem Jesus solves? Where is it? Does it exist between us and evil powers? Is it between us and God? Or is it within ourselves?

There is good biblical evidence to say yes to each of these. In Hebrews we read that Jesus, through his death, intended to "destroy the one who has the power of death . . . and free those who all their lives were held in slavery by the fear of death" (Hebrews 2:14-15). Passages like this make it look as if the main problem is connected to the power of evil. At the end of Romans 4, Paul tells us that Jesus' faith made him righteous, and us as well. He also says that Jesus "was handed over to death for our trespasses and raised for our justification" (v. 25). Paul seems convinced that our trespasses separate us from God, giving credence to the idea that the problem lies between us and our Creator. Yet in the famous passage on God's love in 1 John 4, we get the impression that what God does is demonstrate love through Jesus, a love that we are enabled to imitate. That would seem to address a problem within ourselves. These are all ways of describing how Jesus' story influences our own.

The most ancient postbiblical descriptions of the work of Christ emphasize his victory over the powers of evil. This explanation is often labeled **Christus victor**; it is sometimes referred to as the **classic view**. J. Denny Weaver advocates for recovering an updated version of this approach. One way some early theologians understood the victory of Jesus over evil was that Jesus functioned a bit like bait that God used to trap the devil.

Because of the sin of Adam and Eve, the devil was the rightful lord of human creatures. Since Jesus was human, the devil claimed him and killed him. He took the bait. However, since Jesus was God and couldn't be contained by death, the devil had overreached, and he lost his right to everyone else. Thus Jesus was victorious over the devil, and set us free.

Later on, especially in the work of the medieval theologian Anselm of Canterbury (1033–1109), the emphasis turned to the fractured relationship between human creatures and the Creator. This is the idea that the atonement is about the **satisfaction** of a debt we owed to God. It's known more technically as the **objective model**. It's sometimes described in this way: In sinning against an infinite God, humans accrued an infinite debt. Of course, we couldn't pay it. No finite creature could, and all human creatures, the ones owing the debt, are finite. Except one. Jesus is both human, which means he takes on our debt, and divine, which means he has the infinite resources to pay. An important variation of this idea, especially for Protestants, is the view that humans deserved punishment for breaking God's law. In his suffering and death, Jesus takes this on himself. He becomes our penal substitute in a cosmic courtroom.

Finally, and somewhat in response to this last set of explanations, is the idea of **moral influence**, also known as the **subjective model**. This way of understanding the atonement is connected with a medieval theologian named Peter Abelard (1079–1142). In this view, the main problem is located not between us and God or between us and the powers of evil—it's within ourselves. Jesus provides us with the knowledge and the motivation for acting rightly. Abelard is well known for advocating this sort of an understanding. (He's also famous for falling in love with one of his students, Héloïse. The story is that her uncle was not impressed with the relationship. He was angry, actually—angry enough to hire a group of guys to castrate Abelard. Abelard then became a monk and wrote a book called *A History of My Misfortunes*. It's a title one can understand.)

Maybe this is another area where we don't have to choose between multiple options. If sin is pervasive, and if its effects seep into our relationships with evil powers, with God, with each other, and even with ourselves, then maybe all these ways of describing Jesus' atoning work have their uses. Maybe there isn't one exclusively correct way to explain the significance and meaning of Jesus' life, death, and resurrection. Speaking of what Jesus has done as victory over evil powers shouldn't exclude speaking in other ways in other situations. All of these views have good biblical grounding. What's more, they are all metaphors. God is not literally a judge. God did not use Jesus to literally pay a ransom. We do not literally owe God a great sum of money. Any theory is a description; it is not the thing itself. The thing itself is the actual work of God: the actual multidimensional repair of relationships disrupted by sin.

Choosing not to choose between these ways of describing the atonement doesn't in itself deal with the question of whether God uses violence to address the problem of sin. I happen to think that it isn't possible to read Scripture well and conclude that God is never implicated in violent acts. God's love brings an end to oppression and hatred, but it does so by forcibly ending their power. As creatures culpable for the breaking of shalom, we find ourselves on the wrong side of this. We are not just victims of evil forces but perpetrators as well. For God to lovingly welcome the enslaved and the abused, those who enslave and abuse must feel the force of justice. The beauty of the gospel is found in the fact that God judges and defeats these powers while providing a path forward for those complicit with evil. It is also found in the fact that God identifies with humanity so thoroughly through Jesus that God is not only the one who does the judging but also the one who is judged. Among other places in the New Testament, you can explore this in 2 Timothy 4 and 1 Peter 2.

DEBATING THE MYSTERY

It is one thing to say that Jesus is the fleshly reality of God and is as worthy of worship as the other members of the Trinity. It is another thing to say *how* this is so. It's worth noticing that something being two things at once is more common than we might think. Many of us are someone's child and someone else's parent simultaneously. We can be the second because we are the first. A word is both a physical thing—a set of printed letters, a sound wave, or a hand gesture—and an idea full of meaning. Again, it can be the second because it is the first.

The most significant aspects of this discussion developed within the context of worship. For instance, ancient churches disagreed on whether it was appropriate to refer to Mary as **theotokos**, the bearer of God. The question came down to whether it was possible to speak of Jesus' humanity apart from his divinity. Theologians from two ancient centers of Christian learning approached the matter differently. In Alexandria, Christians tended to speak of Jesus, the Incarnate Word, as having *one* compound nature. In Antioch (in modern-day Turkey), believers tended to say that Jesus had *two* natures. Some of them were so persistent that they spoke of Jesus as being virtually two persons. For these believers, it wouldn't have been appropriate to say that Mary bore God (*theotokos*), because, they would say, she didn't; she bore Christ.

As these communities tried to puzzle through this, the thinking of two people floated to the top of the discussion: Nestorius (386–450), a bishop in Constantinople, and Cyril (376–444), a bishop from Alexandria. Nestorius represented the Antioch perspective. Cyril was a bit like an online troll: he kept bugging Nestorius to clarify his opinion . . . until he went too far. Cyril got Nestorius to say that the two natures in Jesus were basically

a couple: human and divine united by a shared will. Cyril's sup-
porters interpreted this to mean that Nestorius thought the divine
Word was separable from the human Jesus. It was sort of like the
human Jesus did all the compromising stuff—passed through his
mother's birth canal, got hungry, perspired, suffered, died—while
the divine Word hovered above the animal mess, keeping clean
and unaffected. Cyril, on the other hand, seems to have believed
that the human and divine natures were combined into one. I say
seems to have believed because contemporary historians aren't
sure that Cyril really knew what he believed.

As you might expect, this controversy led to another gathering
of church leaders. This was known as the Council of Ephesus,
which occurred in 431. Even though it wasn't in Cyril's hometown, he headed the event. Nestorius and his allies were late in
arriving. They got held up at the airport or something. Cyril began
anyway and—no surprise here—condemned the Nestorian view.
The Nestorians felt put out, and held a rival council condemning
Cyril. As in the days of Nicaea, the emperor tried to negotiate. He
wanted compromise and agreed to exile Nestorius if Cyril would
somehow say that Jesus had two natures. Cyril agreed, affirming
that in Jesus there is one divine person with two natures. He said
the two natures are distinct in theory but not in reality. This was
a happy thought, but it didn't solve anything.

A little more than ten years later, after a fellow named Dioscorus
succeeded Cyril in Alexandria, a monk in Constantinople named
Eutyches came to the attention of the church leaders. Eutyches
believed that it was best to speak of two natures in Jesus, human
and divine, *before* the incarnation but to only speak of one nature
after. He was condemned by a local gathering of leaders and was
exiled. To stoke the debate, Dioscorus offered him sanctuary in
Alexandria and then led another council in Ephesus. This did not
go well. The group that attended was not very representative, and
to make things worse, when someone attempted to read a letter

from the bishop of Rome, he was beaten so badly that he later died. The bishop of Rome, also known as Pope Leo, opposed the view of Eutyches and dismissed the council as a conference of gangsters. The emperor, however, threw his support behind the Alexandrian view—which, if you've lost track, was the view that the human and divine somehow fused together in Jesus. This looked to be the way of the future . . . until the emperor died. Some Christians still attribute his death to divine intervention. However, if God was in the business of knocking off idiots, most of us could hand in a list of better suggestions.

At this point, it wouldn't be crazy to throw up our hands and walk away. In fact, that was basically what I usually argued for during my theological studies. I thought that the whole debate was about power and that the imperial forces were controlling the outcomes. When I began teaching this stuff, I found that most of my students were turned off by the abstraction and precision the ancient leaders wanted. Why does this matter—to us now, to Christians back then? It seems far removed from the Bible and from our spiritual experience. There is good reason for these kinds of responses. Without a doubt, some of the disagreement is little more than bishops wrestling over power. Furthermore, the terms and concepts of the debate don't feel much like the world of the Bible.

My mind has changed a bit on this, though. I've now studied and experienced enough church meetings, small and large, to realize that nothing we do together is ever neat and tidy. We are never free from outside interests or internal manipulation. I know this sounds terrible, but it is the way of things, and it has been this way since the beginning of the faith. There never was a golden age when leaders didn't argue and when there were no factions. Think of the Bible itself. For all that we say about the way we meet God as we read it, and for all that we say about the beauty and truth it contains, it remains a very human book. It is thoroughly awash in cultural assumptions and compromises. It's ugly and violent in places. Remember the "text of terror" from the end of Judges?

I'm more ready now than ever to admit that God works through this stuff. I'm more inclined now to see the ways in which the church leaders subverted the narrow interests of the empire and even called each other out for terrible behavior. If we want a community free of compromise and free of manipulation, we must look beyond the church. We will have to look so far beyond it, however, that we'll end up in a realm with no people at all.

CHALCEDON

If you're not going to remember the specifics of the debates I just outlined, that's fine. But do remember the Council of Nicaea, and do remember what we are about to discuss here, the Council of Chalcedon. Shortly after the death of the emperor Theodosius II, the empress Pulcheria, his younger sister, called for another conference. It happened in Chalcedon, now part of the city of Istanbul, in 451. The council didn't develop a new creed. Instead, the group developed what is known as the **Definition of Chalcedon**, sometimes called the Symbol of Chalcedon. The gathered leaders agreed that it was right to say that Jesus was fully God and fully human. They agreed that he was like us in all things except sin and that he was eternally begotten of God the Father. Further—and this was the critical part—they affirmed that Jesus had both a human and a divine nature, and that these were joined in one person, or in Greek, one *hypostasis*. This joining was such that the two natures were unconfused, unchanged, indivisible, and inseparable.

It's important to notice that this definition does not explain exactly *how* this happened. The leaders of the Christian community were not trying to find a way around the mystery. Instead, they were marking the outer shape of it. The key words—*unconfused, unchanged*, *indivisible*, and *inseparable*—are sometimes referred to as the **four fences** for this reason. Whenever the creaturely and the divine meet, the connection is beyond the capacity of our language. Our words and ideas come from the workings of the world. They can't get at this mysterious connection directly. Chalcedon's fences give shape to the incarnation by telling us what it isn't. Classically, we say this is **apophatic knowledge**—it's a knowledge of what God is not.

It is not critical that every Christian adopt all the philosophical underpinnings of the definition or believe exactly what these bishops believed. Nevertheless, I think the basic Chalcedonian outline is helpful. It helps us talk about the way in which Jesus fully identifies with humans and embodies the very presence of God. It reminds us that the incarnation did not create some kind of hybrid creature that wasn't really divine or human. For Protestants, Chalcedon marks the end of the councils that count. However, some ancient churches in the East thought Chalcedon itself was invalid. These churches continue to speak of Jesus as having one nature. The technical term for this is **monophysitism**. We live with this difference today. Certain church families from North Africa and the Middle East still speak of Jesus as having one nature.

Philosophical dissection is fun and imaginative for some. For others of us, stories say more. On the theme of Jesus' identity, there may be none more powerful than the one told by twentieth-century Japanese novelist Shūsaku Endō. His book *Silence* tells the story of a young Jesuit priest named Sebastão Rodrigues, who ministered in Japan in the mid-seventeenth century. At that time, Christians were being persecuted, and many practiced their faith in secret. The authorities devised a plan to figure out who they were. They rounded up suspected Christians and made them step on a carved image of Jesus. Those who refused to dishonor the image were sent to prison.

Sebastão Rodrigues is captured and forced to watch as other Christians are tortured and killed. He had assumed that martyrdom would be a glorious event. However, all he sees is pain. Eventually, the authorities begin torturing lay Christians specifically to get priests like Rodrigues to step on the figure of Jesus. This creates a deep dilemma for Rodrigues, one that you can't fully appreciate without reading Endō's book, but that I'll summarize here. Should the priest renounce his faith to save the peasants he served? It would be selfish not to, wouldn't it? Or should he honor Jesus by refusing to step on the carving? The story reaches its climax when Rodrigues hears the image of Christ speak to him: "Trample! Trample! I more than anyone know of the pain in your foot. Trample! It was to be trampled on by men that I was born into this world. It was to share men's pain that I carried my cross."[2]

The Definition of Chalcedon says some important things about the mystery of the incarnation, but it doesn't say everything. The most crucial thing—the thing we must not miss and the thing Endō's story captures—is that the incarnation reveals a God whose grace upsets our assumptions about divinity, a God who shares our pain.

14

THEY WERE ALL TOGETHER *in* ONE PLACE

Connections

We believe in one holy catholic and apostolic church.
—**Nicene Creed**

I was sitting in a coffee shop on campus one afternoon when one of my students sat down and started talking about a verse from John 5. In the passage Jesus is speaking to religious leaders who criticized him for healing a man who had been ill for decades. Jesus had healed him on the Sabbath. That was the problem. In verse 39, Jesus says, "You search the scriptures because you think that in them you have eternal life; and it is they that testify on my behalf." My student, a former lumberjack, said, "It's great that we talk about the Bible so much, but I'm starting to wonder if we're overdoing it. What if I memorized the whole thing? So what?" He was right. He went on to say that he was learning that studying Scripture is a means to an end. The end is to encounter the God we know in Jesus. That's the core of the Christian life: encountering God and being refashioned by the gracious power of the Spirit.

God, like the Waldo character in the children's books, can sometimes be hard to find. Yes, it's easy to find references to God in the Bible, but that's not what I'm getting at. What I mean is that God is hard to find precisely because our expectations are so high. Christians believe Jesus is alive and on the loose. We believe he has sent the Spirit to sustain us. "Where can I go from your spirit?" the poet asks in Psalm 139. "Where can I flee from your presence? If I ascend to heaven, you are there; if I make my bed in Sheol, you are there" (vv. 7-8). What we expect isn't just to read about God or to hear people speak about the Trinity. We expect to encounter God as a living, interactive being. One of the reasons we use the language of Father, Son, and Spirit is that these terms denote personhood in ways that most of their substitutes do not.

Jesus left his students. After the resurrection, some meals with the disciples, and a minor medical probe from Thomas, Jesus left. That's what the story of the ascension in Luke 24 and Acts 1 describes. Jesus, Emmanuel, God with us—leaves. Acts says a "cloud took him out of their sight" (Acts 1:9). Although Jesus is no longer present in person, the Christian spiritual tradition claims that we still have access to him through the cloud.

I could be wrong about this, but I think there are two main ways we connect with God: through prayer and through the church. After Jesus' ascension the disciples returned to Jerusalem and devoted themselves to prayer. Prayer is the central Christian spiritual practice. There are many other important practices, like hospitality, worship, generosity, sharing in communion, baptism, preaching, and yes, studying Scripture. These practices are essential to the Christian life, but they are all undergirded by prayer. British theologian Sarah Coakley suggests that theology itself begins with prayer. She says this—brace yourself—"The practice of prayer provides the context in which silence in the Spirit expands the potential to respond to the realm of the Word."[1] You may want to read that line twice. Coakley's point is that trinitarian thinking is linked to prayer and participation in worship in community. Prayer knits our theological speech with the experience of God. It makes conversations about theology more than vocabulary exercises.

PRAYER AND OTHER LINKS

The library at the small college where I had taken a teaching position held only a fraction of the volumes in the enormous collection I had access to in Toronto. Prayer was something I had practiced for years, but I had never thought about it purposefully. As a new college professor, I was finding that the pace of my life was picking up. Still in my twenties, I felt as if I had jumped into the deep end of the pool. I prayed as I traveled to and from campus. As I walked and biked around campus, I found that the natural world prompted me to meditate on certain characteristics of God, and I would find myself praying for students and colleagues. This fluid approach to prayer left me feeling a bit guilty. Was it a spiritual practice if it wasn't at least a little more . . . disciplined? It wasn't too long before I found myself drifting through the section in the library with books on prayer and the spiritual life. I noticed that the name of a Spanish mystical theologian, Teresa of Ávila (1515–82), kept popping up.

Ávila, Teresa's birthplace is just about in the middle of modern-day Spain. Teresa's mother died when the future mystic was still young. Teresa's father was strict, and the young woman found an escape in popular books and an active social life. Teresa's father sent her to a convent school. I can't imagine that it always works out this way, but for Teresa this actually did lead to a deeper spiritual life—so deep, in fact, that she officially entered a Carmelite monastery in 1535. The spiritual climate of the monastery was not terribly earnest, though, and this frustrated her. There were more than one hundred nuns, but the spiritual companionship she had hoped for didn't materialize. Prayer seemed less important to these women than connecting with the wealthy and influential. So in 1562 Teresa started a reformed Carmelite community. She and her companions would be "discalced"—that is, they would be barefoot. Teresa convinced her friend, whom we know as John of the Cross (1542–91), to lead a community of men practicing the same strict spiritual discipline. John was so serious about his commitment to God that when he discerned at one point that he was becoming overly attached to Teresa, he burned all the letters she had sent him.

During the time I was getting to know Teresa, I noticed that one of my students wore shoes only when absolutely necessary. It was an uncanny connection. He too felt called to the spiritual discipline of going barefoot. And this was Canada, not Spain, so I was impressed. One way to understand the contribution of people like Teresa of Ávila, John of the Cross, and another Spaniard named Ignatius of Loyola (1491–1556) is to notice that they were pursuing church reform at roughly the same time as those in the north who would eventually be known as Protestants. Putting it that way reminds us that Protestantism and Catholicism are not totally distinct forms of faith. The life of the Catholic Church before the sixteenth-century split is also the heritage of those of us who are Protestants. The ancient church is our church; the medieval church is our church.

The key distinction between the southern Reformers and those from the north was that the former didn't end up separated from their mother church. It's true that Teresa was frustrated with the spiritual laxity of the monastic community she joined. Around the same time, other believers were frustrated with the influence of money on the church in general. In some instances people could buy church positions for themselves or for their friends. This was known as **simony**, named after the biblical character Simon who, in Acts 8, tried to buy the Spirit's power. In many places, clergy were not very skilled or committed, and many couldn't preach well. Some couldn't read. They thought their job was mostly to offer the sacraments, even though average Christians were often not allowed to fully participate in communion. It became difficult for those who weren't ordained or weren't monks to know how to live their faith. Mostly it seemed they were just supposed to follow the church's orders, even when the leaders seemed to be taking advantage of them.

Part of the practice of pastoral care in the late medieval period was something called **penance**. When someone confessed a sin, they were given an assignment, something that was supposed to make things right or at least help them heal. Say you stole your neighbor's axe. Eventually, because you were worried about the long-term effects of your sin, you told your priest. He told you to either give your neighbor a new axe or chop all her wood for a year. If things couldn't be repaired, the priest might just tell you to do a certain number of prayers to heal your soul. The belief was that what you didn't make right in this life God would have to rectify later. This was what **purgatory** was all about: purging you of sin. It was in the context of this practice that the church also sold indulgences. An **indulgence** was, more or less, a certificate awarded for good deeds or for penance you had done. It could lessen the time needed to make amends for your sins.

One way to receive an indulgence was by donating to the church building fund, or to the fund for the bishop's vacation home. You could even purchase an indulgence on behalf of a dead loved one. Some indulgence salesmen—Johan Tetzel is the best example—became famous. Tetzel was pretty slick. For some Catholics, like the Augustinian monk we've met before named Martin Luther, the sale of indulgences was symptomatic of a deeper problem. Luther thought faith in God's grace had been eclipsed by faith in one's religious practice. Spiritual practices like prayer had become more like duties than gifts. This was possible, Luther and his fellow Reformers believed, because the church had made its own tradition more authoritative than Scripture.

It wasn't just church stuff that led to the Protestant Reformation. There were political factors, like the breakup of vast empires, and cultural factors, like the rise of **humanism**. Humanism was a new intellectual mood that emphasized independent thinking and a return to original biblical, philosophical, and literary sources. It downplayed the need for conservative hierarchies and tradition. The development of the printing press and the rise in literacy also made the continent ripe for the spread of ideas. In 1517 Martin Luther nailed his Ninety-Five Theses to the door of All Saints' Church in Wittenberg. He intended to have a debate about the validity of indulgences. His theses, or points of debate, were quickly translated from Latin, the language of scholars, to German. They were printed up and sent across the continent. The results cascaded over the following decades. Eventually, Luther and his followers were no longer welcome in the Roman Catholic Church; the resulting fracture led to a whole panoply of Protestant churches. For Protestant insiders, it can be tempting to think of the Reformation as a triumph for some particular brand of Christianity. The reality is that it led to Christians using violence, even torture and death, against other Christians. Theological differences were combined with political instability to produce wars. It's hard to look back and cheer when these things were among the results.

The main body of Protestant Reformers worked hand in hand with various civil authorities, so we call them **Magisterial**

Reformers. We describe the loose network of those who didn't cooperate with governing authorities as **Radical Reformers.** Although their leaders met on occasion, most communities of the Radical Reformation were led locally. Today, certain church networks, including Baptists and many Pentecostals, follow this precedent. Some of the key early leaders in this tribe were Menno Simons, an ex-priest, and Michael Sattler (1495–1527), an ex-monk. Unlike the Magisterial Reformers, few leaders of the Radical Reformation had the training or the leisured safety to write much formal theology. Although Menno Simons did write some, he's best known simply for the fact that modern Mennonites bear his name.

One of the Roman Catholic Church's responses to the Protestants was to launch what we now call the Counter-Reformation. New religious orders were started and existing ones were reformed. Seminaries were founded to train priests. Officially, the Counter-Reformation came to a head with the Council of Trent. It began in 1545 and reconvened periodically for nearly two decades. It did nothing to heal the rift with the Protestants. The rift between Protestants and Catholics remains, officially at least, to our own time.

One hopeful sign, though, is the growing appreciation among Protestants for the writings of Catholic spiritual teachers like Teresa, John of the Cross, and Ignatius of Loyola. Teresa's most well-known work is called *The Interior Castle*. In it she depicts the spiritual life as a movement through seven mansions within a castle. The metaphor was close at hand for her. The city of Ávila itself was walled, and Teresa lived much of her life within a walled monastery. The way to enter the spiritual life, she said, was through prayer. True prayer isn't just silent contemplation or mindless words. It certainly isn't telling God what to do. True prayer is humble. It is accompanied by a detachment from the things of the world that distort our desire for our true Beloved.

Prayer moves us through various stages of the spiritual life. One of the things we learn as we grow in the life of prayer is that love is more important than having immense knowledge.

Part of the significance of Teresa's work was that her focus, the inner life of prayer, was beyond the control of church structures. Despite her spiritual maturity, Teresa could not become a priest or a bishop. Women were leaders in the early days of the faith, when they served as deacons in local congregations and as patrons of important churches. However, across the centuries, roles in the church had become more tightly defined, and women were largely excluded from official leadership roles. The influence on the church by someone like Teresa had to come in sideways, so she wrote about prayer. The mansion at the center of the castle symbolizes union with the divine Beloved. It symbolizes seeing clearly the three persons of the Trinity through the eyes of the soul. We can wonder what could be more influential than that.

COMMUNITY

The school where I taught was part of the very global but very informal evangelical network. The strength of the school was its global consciousness, rooted in Christian service and mission. Kwame Bediako says that, at its best, the missionary encounter is not what happens when an "advanced" culture hands out spiritual insights to one that is more "primitive." Christian mission is what happens when our sense of meaning, spirituality, and culture encounters Jesus.[2] The encounter is an opportunity, a gift given with an open hand and without a predetermined outcome. However, the besetting weaknesses of many evangelical institutions were also present in the school where I taught. There was a lack of historical consciousness and an overriding sense that true faith was identical to an emotional experience. Things like this can lead to spiritual arrogance. Companions like Teresa became immensely important to me.

I had taken the job—and chosen to leave the life of a full-time student—because I wanted to see if the stuff I had been studying meshed with the lives of people who had no intention of becoming professional theologians or church leaders. I wanted to know if it would give them a compelling way of speaking about life. I suggested earlier that prayer and the church are the two main ways we connect with God. The church involves worship and splendid conversations with friends, but it is more than that. The church is where we learn to speak about God. It's the place where our lives are refashioned into the form of Jesus.

The part of the theological conversation in which we discuss the church is known as **ecclesiology**. *Ecclesia* is one of the Greek words from the New Testament translated into English as "church." In 1 Corinthians, Paul gives a long description of the Christian community as a body with different parts. In the body there are hands and eyes, feet and ears. Each one is important for the body's functioning. Being a part of the Christian community, the church, means that we all bring different gifts and abilities. What we sometimes miss in this passage is this line: "You are the body of Christ and individually members of it" (1 Corinthians 12:27). This group of strivers and failures, of the wrecked and the celebrated—these people make up Christ's corporeal presence here and now. I'm pretty sure it was the long-haired Lutheran theologian Robert Jenson who suggested we stop thinking of this as a metaphor: the church *is* Christ's body.

Many Protestants, following John Calvin, identify the church as the community where the Word is rightly preached and where the sacraments are rightly administered. Calvin's heirs would expand on this to describe the church as a covenant community. Heirs of Luther would speak more readily of the church as a community of justified sinners. Others, especially Pentecostals, would say that we can recognize the church by the obvious presence of the gifts of the Holy Spirit. Pentecostals are part of a larger charismatic movement, which emphasizes the need to recover spiritual gifts like prophecy and speaking in tongues. The modern charismatic movement began in the twentieth century, and has become the fastest growing branch of Christianity anywhere. Anabaptist Christians, close relatives of Pentecostals—older cousins, maybe—would say that we recognize the church as a community of people who act like Jesus. Both Anabaptists and Pentecostals link themselves with the earliest incarnations of the church and have traditionally been critical of the church in between.

Distinct from Protestants, Orthodox and Catholic Christians place a stronger emphasis on the institutional character of the church. For Orthodox Christians, the church serves as an icon of the Trinity. The relationships of individual congregations to the whole reflects the relationships of Father, Son, and Spirit. The institutional character of Catholicism is more hierarchical. Catholics see the church quite strongly as the people of God, a people whose identity stems from its leaders and their links through the ages to Peter.

In the mid-twentieth century, Catholic leaders gathered at the Vatican in Rome for another official council. It would be known as Vatican II. The question they gathered to discuss was not the doctrine of the Trinity or the dual natures of Jesus: it was the relationship of the church to the modern world. One of the important documents the council produced is known as *Lumen Gentium*. The title comes from the first two words of the original Latin text. Several lines from the first paragraph of the second chapter express an important aspect of modern Catholic ecclesiology:

> At all times and in every race God has given welcome to whosoever fears Him and does what is right (Acts 10:35). God, however, does not make men holy and save them merely as individuals, without bond or link between one another. Rather has it pleased Him to bring men together as one people, a people which acknowledges Him in truth and serves Him in holiness.[3]

Protestants are more inclined, probably to a fault, to describe the faith as an individual pursuit. One of the gifts Catholics bring to their Protestant brothers and sisters is this sense of community and peoplehood. Being a Christian means joining the people of God.

I remember a student approaching me at an informal evening barbecue on the first day of a new academic year. She probably didn't know how new I was to the job. She asked me what I thought the Bible had to say about God knowing the future. That sparked a conversation between us that ran through her graduation and beyond. Many of the students I got to know were pretty serious about the Bible. The school's administrators were too. Yet in that context there was almost—and I wish I had a better way of putting it—a "magical" view of the Bible. The sense was that more of the Bible was always better, as though any question could be answered with just one quick finger-walk from relevant verse to relevant verse. When we are honest, most of us know that we can't read the Bible well without the help of others. The fact that we are tempted to go it alone, that we sometimes overlook our need for hermeneutical formation, is part of the Reformation's legacy.

Luther had tried to be the perfect penitent. He tried to do everything within his power to improve his standing before God. Unlike Teresa of Ávila, though, he could only move forward by moving beyond the Catholic theology he knew. Near the beginning of 1 Corinthians, Paul says that he made a firm decision to know nothing "except Jesus Christ, and him crucified" (1 Corinthians 2:2). Luther latched on to this. It symbolized his own rejection of the ambitions of medieval Christianity.

Although Reformers like Teresa and Luther are the ones whose names show up on library shelves, they drew on earlier movements and literature. In northern Europe a renewal movement called the Devotio Moderna flourished during the fifteenth century. The theology of the communities associated with this movement is symbolized by *The Imitation of Christ*, a little book by Thomas à Kempis (1380–1471). As the book's title suggests, this new devotion prioritized humility and service. In England, John Wycliffe (1330–84) was another important precursor of the Reformation. He is sometimes referred to as "the morning star of the Reformation." Wycliffe translated the Bible into the local language instead of leaving it in Latin, the language of scholars and church leaders. Wycliffe also advocated for the disentanglement of church and state structures. He was deeply critical of the sale of indulgences. There was also the Czech priest Jan Hus (1369–1415), who kept alive Wycliffe's arguments. The work of these pre-Reformation figures was not universally appreciated. Some four decades after Wycliffe's death, his corpse was dug up and burned, and the ashes thrown in the river. Hus was chained to a stake and burned. The combined authorities of church and state were zealous to protect their power.

We often want to separate ourselves from this messy history. Many of us want to cut ourselves off from anything that seems formal or institutional. We're modern folks, and we don't like the idea of being saddled with the debts of previous generations. It's tempting to think we can follow Jesus without connecting ourselves to the historical church. This is impossible. We wouldn't have the Bible without the historical church. The church's mixed record is an inheritance that comes with the good news it carries. There is no knowledge of Jesus without the church transmitting it through time and across space. There are no Scriptures without the church. There are no sages of Christian prayer without the church. As we learn to pray in the church, we learn to repent for the ways we have broken shalom and for the times the church has too.

15

EAT THIS BREAD
and DRINK THIS CUP

Practices

Just as a tree cannot bear fruit if it is often transplanted, so neither can a monk bear fruit if he frequently changes his abode.
—Ancient Christian monk

You might have gathered that the Reformation is becoming a tricky thing for Christians to talk about. I say "becoming" because in previous generations, Catholics and Protestants believed each other to not be true Christians. That made things easy, in a way. Those who left one team and joined the other spoke about their conversions as movement from error to truth. Each stream viewed the figures in their own history as heroes and those of the other as villains. It may not have been very generous or historically sensitive, but it was clear.

Near the end of my time as a theology teacher, I was granted several months of sabbatical leave. The point of a luxury like this is to allow faculty to do things that contribute to their work that they normally can't do. My family and I decided to spend the time near a Catholic monastery. We would be part of an institute where professors, pastors, writers, and artists lived in community. We would discuss our work with each other, share some meals, and trade some insights. I was looking forward to that part of the experience. My family was looking forward to exploring a place with lots of lakes and trees. On the prairies where we lived, we were missing trees, especially oaks and towering pines. The place we were headed to had them both.

I had anticipated that it would be good to spend time with others who were engaged in writing projects, and I wanted to work on developing a theological understanding of modern technology. What I didn't expect was how intriguing it would be to be close to a monastery. Protestants talk a good game about prayer, but these monks put down their work four times a day to do it. Protestants have a lot to say about valuing the Bible, but these black-robed fellows had commissioned a massive project to create a Bible the way it was done during medieval times. It was made of velum and spanned several volumes. It had vivid contemporary illuminations made from traditional pigments. The words of the text were penned by hand, by calligraphers using actual feather pens. People by the busload made pilgrimages to see the final product. The book even starred in documentaries.

These monks were certainly not perfect. Like that of the church at large, their history is riddled with mistakes. Even so, it was fascinating to be on the periphery of a community whose spirituality so clearly balanced the goodness of work and prayer. While I was there, in addition to my research and writing, I spent time in prayer about the next steps for my family and me. We were planning to move, and I was considering a pastoral appointment. A monk in his nineties had an office near mine. He was an ordained priest and a recognized theologian. I thought that if anyone could speak to the relationship of theological scholarship and pastoral ministry, it would be him.

This is the point where you might expect me to recount some gem of an idea an old monk proffered. The monk was very kind, but he didn't have much advice. What was significant, though, was that I was there and that I could consider him a helpful example. It was a testament to changing relationship between Protestants and Catholics. We now recognize each other as Christians. We ask each other for advice. We're inclined to see each other's gifts, not just each other's faults.

WHAT THE CHURCH DOES

One of the things I grew to value about the monastic community was the sense that they were buckled in for the long haul. Their old buildings had been made of good brick, their furniture of oak. They planned in blocks of hundreds of years. The evangelical college where I taught put up buildings quickly. Some of their older ones were insulated with newspaper and sawdust. They were in a hurry. I liked certain things about the monks' worship too. It was tactile. There was always stuff to touch and taste and smell.

Christian communities do many things, but most centrally they worship. In worship there is prayer, sung praise, and the reading of Scripture. Out of worship comes hope, service, and love for those Jesus calls "the least of these." Since the church's beginning, the **sacraments**, the rituals and practices of the church, have been central. They have been central not just to the church's worship but also to its entire life. As we discussed earlier, the church's sacramental practices grow out of the biblical theme of God's presence in the world. This presence was marked by physical symbols. Ancient Israel on the move through the desert could be confident of God's presence as signaled by the cloud and the fire. Later, the temple took on that role. Then there was Jesus himself, God present in human flesh.

Local churches continue this sacramental presence. To be a church is to be a community where people encounter God's presence. Sometimes these divine encounters happen informally. Maybe some members visit those who are sick as a sign of God's care. Maybe while in conversation about a challenging situation we get the sense that God is speaking to us through the words of friends or enemies. Work done on behalf of those who have little power shows that God loves them. These Christ-shaped things are signs that God's Spirit is breathing new life into a weary world.

Not all sacramental signs are informal. In fact, the primary ones are regular and have deep historical roots. Baptism and communion are the best examples. These are things that Jesus commanded his followers to do. When Jesus broke bread and shared it with his disciples, he said, "Do this in remembrance of me" (Luke 22:19). At the end of Matthew, Jesus commissioned his disciples, telling them, "Go therefore and make disciples of all nations, baptizing them in the name of the Father and of the Son and of the Holy Spirit" (Matthew 28:19). During the Reformation, one of the key debates centered on the nature of these practices. Were they simply symbols—nice ways to remember what Jesus did—or was God still doing something through them?

The most famous back and forth on the nuts and bolts of the sacramental machinery occurred between Martin Luther and a Swiss reformer named Ulrich Zwingli (1484–1531). I once had a Swiss couple in one of my classes. They cheered when I mentioned Zwingli. Apparently he's quite a hero in Switzerland. Zwingli died defending Zurich in battle. As you would expect, Zwingli is considered a Magisterial Reformer. He worked hand in hand with civil magistrates and created something much like a theocracy, a government run by religious leaders.

A list of Magisterial Reformers would include leaders we've discussed already, namely Luther, Zwingli, and Calvin, but also the early leaders of the Church of England, including Thomas Cranmer (1489–1556) and Richard Hooker (1554–1600). Anglicans around the world today, and Episcopalians in the United States, trace their roots to the Reformation in England. Anglicanism tries to walk a middle path between Protestantism and Catholicism. You probably already know the story of Henry VIII, but it was really the middle way, the *via media*, promoted by Elizabeth I that shaped the core of Anglicanism. Under her watch the Church of England kept the Book of Common Prayer, which Cranmer had compiled, as well as formal liturgy and an episcopal polity. Anglicans would keep those things that, to other Protestants, seem very "Catholic." Yet they would remain separate from Roman Catholicism. If you aren't used to traditional liturgy, most Anglican churches you might stumble into today would feel Catholic. Yet Anglicans grant authority to Scripture over tradition, as other Protestants do. They let their priests marry. They generally try to follow Hooker's lead in not prescribing too many theological details.

All the Magisterial Reformers had access to coercive power. Thus the English monarch is called the "Defender of the Faith" and is officially the head of the Church of England. Thus John Calvin famously advocated for killing the freethinking Michael Servetus. Servetus was burned alive. Thus Zwingli actively promoted the torture and killing of the Anabaptists. The Anabaptists, considered Radical Reformers, represent a different political vision. They rejected the idea that secular power should be used in matters of faith. The movement officially began in 1525 when a man named George Blaurock, who had been baptized as an infant, asked to be baptized as an adult. In his mind it wasn't rebaptism; he considered it his first real baptism. For his involvement in the movement, Blaurock was tortured and burned at the stake. Beyond the issue of baptism, the Anabaptists can be distinguished from other Protestants because of their emphasis on **regeneration**, a change in the way one lives, over **justification**, a change in one's standing before God. The most obvious outworking of this distinction may be the Anabaptist commitment to nonviolence, a practice grounded in the assumption that Jesus' teaching about loving one's neighbor and one's enemy has practical, this-worldly implications. This emphasis on regeneration is one of the ways in which the Anabaptists were more like their Catholic grandparents than their Lutheran parents.

The difference between Zwingli and Luther, which I alluded to earlier, wasn't about civil government. The two mostly agreed on that. They certainly disagreed with the Anabaptists. Zwingli and Luther disagreed about how we should talk about the sacraments, especially about communion. Zwingli was convinced that when Jesus described the bread as his body, he was obviously speaking in metaphorical terms. Luther disagreed.

This difference over how we understand the sacraments runs through the global church even now. On the one side are those who believe that something happens to us through these practices. Methodists believe, for instance, that when we are baptized, something actually changes. John Wesley taught that baptism did away with the guilt of original sin. Many people know that Roman Catholics believe the bread and wine of the eucharist undergo a change in their inner substance to become the body and blood of Jesus. This view, called **transubstantiation**, was officially adopted by the Catholic Church at the Council of Trent. It's a clear example of an understanding of a sacrament as being more than a symbol or a reminder.

On the other side of the issue, if we must speak of sides, are most Baptists and Anabaptists, including Mennonite communities like the one I'm a part of now. They stand firmly with Zwingli in thinking of these things as symbols and reminders. The Baptist tradition, which I haven't said much about yet, began in the seventeenth century when John Smyth (1554–1612), a dissenter from the Church of England, encountered Anabaptist communities in Amsterdam. Typically, Baptists and Anabaptists don't think much goes on during communion other than our own solemn remembering of Jesus' love for us unto death. They don't think much goes on in baptism other than the individual's statement of faith. As someone who now regularly leads a congregation in the celebration of communion, I think God's grace flows within and underneath the church's sacramental practices. I think Jesus is present with us in our gathered community. He is there in our remembering, in our being enlivened by the Spirit, and in our following his example.

Most Protestants affirm two sacraments, baptism and communion, while modern Catholics affirm five more: anointing the sick, confession, marriage, holy orders, and confirmation. There is, though, an ancient theological stream that says we don't need to clearly define a list of sacraments. Lots of practices can be sacramental, since they are visible signs of God's grace. That's more or less how Augustine defined a sacrament—"a visible sign of an invisible grace." I find this compelling. Preaching can be a sacrament. So can spiritual direction. Funerals can be sacraments too. When a funeral is done well, we receive the grace of knowing that life and death are in God's hands. We are enabled to say goodbye to someone we love and to glimpse that person's life as an entirety wrapped up in God's care.

A COMMUNITY SET APART

In the last chapter I mentioned that one of the Greek words used in the New Testament to describe the Christian community is *ecclesia*. The word suggests people called out from the masses for some specific reason, maybe for political deliberation or something like that. Christian communities have always had the sense, in one way or another, that they are called out, that they are distinct communities. They are called from the world to advance God's work of reconciliation. Randy Woodley, a theologian and legal descendent of the United Keetoowah Band of Cherokee Indians in Oklahoma, likes to describe this as furthering the "Harmony Way." That is, part of what it means to be the church is to be a people tasked with extending God's peace, the gift of harmony or shalom, in a world amped up on competition and wracked by resentment.[1]

One of the parts of the church that has helped us remember this set-apartness are the monastic communities. These come in all shapes and sizes, Protestant and Catholic. The monastic community I got to know during my sabbatical was Benedictine. That means they followed the Rule of Benedict. In this case, a *rule* simply means a pattern of life. Before Benedict of Nursia (480–547), the most influential monk was probably Anthony of the Desert (251–356). (I sometimes accidentally spell the last part of his name with a double *s*. That gives a very different impression about the man.) According to Benedict, a monk's goal is simply to "lead a life worthy of God." That phrase is borrowed from the second chapter of Paul's first letter to the church in Thessalonica. It's an encouragement to us all.

In the fifth century, Benedict, along with his sister Scholastica (480–543), breathed new life into the monastic tradition sparked by Anthony. They established a time-tested pattern of community life, one that called participants to prayer and work. It encouraged them to periodic silent contemplation and meditation on spiritual texts. It encouraged hospitality. One of the reasons Benedict's Rule has been so influential is its moderation. When Benedict lived, there were monks who were trying to survive only on water, bread, and salt. He encouraged those in his community to enjoy things like wine and meat. Benedict believed that monastic communities should be places where people learn love.

We sometimes think of life in our church communities simply as preparation for the real work of ministering to the poor or sharing the good news that Jesus has defeated the powers of sin and death. We would do better to realize that life in community is itself a part of God's redemptive mission. It is there that lives are reshaped, and it is there that we praise God as creatures were meant to do.

Although people like Benedict, Scholastica, and Anthony are considered leading lights of ancient Christian monasticism, these types of communities have much older roots. That's one of the reasons we shouldn't dismiss them too quickly. In Numbers 6 we read about Nazarites, who symbolized their unique calling from God by not drinking wine and by not cutting their hair. The Essenes, famous for preserving biblical texts, were similar. As odd as it sounds, it was the mainstream acceptance of the Christian faith that led to the growth of monastic communities. Women and men sought remote places and intentional communities to seriously engage God. Members of monastic communities did and still do take vows, often of celibacy or obedience or poverty. That might seem exotic, but in reality the lives of all Christians are shaped by vows. There are vows of baptism or confirmation, vows of membership in a specific church community, and vows of marriage. These vows are flickers or traces of the covenants that run throughout the Bible. It's the commitment and permanence which these vows imply that makes them useful for our growth into the image of Jesus. This is especially true today, when many of us are free to move about as we please. Moving around and ending and beginning relationships are often our ways of avoiding the difficult gift of God's sanctifying grace. This is the grace that will not let us remain selfish creatures in the line of the old Adam.

This is all a bit of what it means to be a set-apart community. Being set apart or called out also means that the Christian community has its own way of making decisions and using power. It stands outside the other institutional networks of society. When it's working well, the church is an odd entity. It has its own sense of what it means to live well. This is why we say that a Christian community is a political entity. Christian communities do not become political when they start talking about elections. They are political when they welcome the poor and when they gather together across racial, ethnic, and social lines. Jesus' disciples didn't always understand this, which is why he was once asked if a certain disciple could be his second-in-command. Jesus was exasperated. In Matthew 20 he says, "You know that the rulers of the Gentiles lord it over them, and their great ones are tyrants over them. It will not be so among you; but whoever wishes to be great among you must be your servant" (vv. 25-26). Leadership and power don't function the same way in the church as they do elsewhere, or at least they shouldn't.

Power is held and symbolized differently across Christian traditions. For instance, Benedictine monks are led by an elected superior called an abbot. When the bishop visits, he sits on a throne. The throne business shows us just how different Christian communities can be from each other, even though they all seek to follow Jesus' example of servant leadership. We say that denominations led by bishops have an **episcopal** polity. A bishop symbolizes the whole church, which is why a bishop sometimes gets to sit on a throne. Denominations led by a council of pastors and elders have a **presbyterian** polity. Some of these pastors wear collars or robes when they lead services. This is to symbolize their priestly role and their bearing the yoke of Jesus. A third type of polity is **congregational**. As you might expect, the idea here is that the whole congregation holds decision-making power. These churches have no special seats and no special uniforms, at least not officially.

Each of these models traces its way of handling things back to the ancient church. In Scripture we read about bishops, pastors, and deacons but also about teachers, evangelists, apostles, prophets, and elders. Every way of organizing a community and exercising power has strengths and weaknesses. What's crucial is that our communities are transparent, accountable, open to God's leading, and open to recognizing the gifts of each member.

A SACRAMENTAL WAY OF LIFE

One of the things I appreciated about the monks I got to know on my sabbatical was the closeness of prayer and work in their lives. Prayer and labor brushed up against each other, rubbed shoulders. Some of the monks worked in a woodshop, others helped manage the land the community owned. In an earlier time they had a farm and ran a college. I met a master potter who lived and worked in the vicinity of the abbey. He went to prayer sometimes. He said he couldn't have done his work in any context other than one like that.

James K. A. Smith, a philosopher and public intellectual, once described a practice among his group of friends. They shared a meal together every week. They paid careful attention to the food they ate and the wine they drank. They called it a "shadow Eucharist." They consciously allowed the meal to remind them of one of the church's core sacraments.[2] It's an example of how the church's core sacramental practices can help us see God's goodness and grace in everyday things like doing work and sharing meals. Bathing can be a shadow of baptism, which is the outward symbol of God's cleansing grace. Food, which almost always requires the death of living organisms, reminds us of God's self-giving. Food also reminds us that our lives—pleasant or painful as they may be—are gifts. Our committed relationships refer us to God's faithfulness, both to ancient Israel and to us. There's no need for us to put church in one day and "secular" life in the other six. Our corporate worship should remind us that our lives belong to God and that they unfold in a good and blessed place. Sunday worship, or whatever day we set aside, gives us the language to describe the transcendent source of life and gives us words to name the evils that plague our world and each of us.

In a previous chapter I described how the church's sense of mission has sometimes caused its members to participate in projects that have harmed those to whom they sought to minister. Our discussion in this chapter reminds us that the challenge is deepened by the fact that the church has also harmed its own members. During the Reformation, opposing churches sanctioned violence against each other. They told their members to tear other Christians' flesh and to torture them. However, in the fourth chapter of his letter to the Ephesians, Paul says that just as there is one God and one baptism, so there is only "one body." That makes our history all the more hideous, if it can possibly be so. It's one body tearing at itself. There's no way to neatly hide this or make it go away or say it doesn't matter. It does matter, and it was sinful. For this reason, it just may be that the greatest gift we receive is the opportunity to confess and repent. It's true for us corporately and true for us individually. Through the church, we receive the language and the consistent prompting that makes regular confession possible.

16

The **FRUIT** *of the* **SPIRIT**

Character

The world of nature, cut off from the source of life, is a dying world. For one who thinks food in itself is the source of life, eating is communion with the dying world, it is communion with death. Food itself is dead, it is life that has died and it must be kept in refrigerators like a corpse.
—Alexander Schmemann

David Foster Wallace, a writer and brilliant observer of culture, once told a graduating class that "learning how to think really means learning how to exercise some control over how and what you think. It means being conscious and aware enough to choose what you pay attention to and to choose how you construct meaning from experience."[1] Wallace's comments are a little narcissistic, but the basic thrust is that we should take an active role in what we think about and how we see the world.

Either we do it ourselves or the murky currents of the broader culture—popular religion, the entertainment industry, government, or whatever—do it for us. If we are carried by these currents we will simply become consumers. Consumers are beings who, for the good of someone else's balance sheet, are persuaded to give up real pleasure to buy stuff they don't need.

One way to get at the issue is to look to Galatians 5, the second to last chapter of Paul's letter to the Galatians. There he sets up a contrast between the things that are produced by the flesh and those things that are produced by the Spirit. Just so we don't misinterpret this, it's important to know that Paul isn't setting up a split between body and spirit, in which the first is sinful and the second is pure. That would be a gnostic view, not a Christian one. Paul says that the things produced by our lower selves are things like idolatry, dividing into factions, envy, infighting, fornication—that sort of stuff. The character produced by the Spirit, he tells us, is love, joy, peace, patience, kindness, generosity, faithfulness, gentleness, and self-control.

We grow in our character through engagement with things beyond ourselves. Sometimes these are literally things: working on an old car can teach us patience, caring for plants can make us aware of our tendency to obsess over ourselves. Nevertheless, for most of us, growth in the Christian virtues Paul mentions comes through being with other people. Even just figuring out how to remain friends with someone over a lifetime requires us to grow in self-control and faithfulness. Several years after I began teaching, I became a parent. Never before had I realized how selfish I could be, or how my anger could slip out in little ways. Caring for a totally (in)dependent little life can make those things obvious. Walking slowly while holding a child's hand can be either blissful or absolutely maddening.

A wonderful description of the early church appears near the end of Acts 2, where we read that the new believers "devoted themselves to the apostles' teaching" (v. 42). Clearly, there was a set of things for them to believe. But the verse quickly adds that they were also devoted to fellowship and to breaking bread and to prayer. There, once again, is the significance of the church and prayer. The early Christians described in Acts had repented of an old life. Their lives had been reoriented and they had been baptized. Like the woman in Luke 13 who had been hunched over by disease and whom Jesus enabled to stand up straight, these early believers had experienced God's grace and were able to stand upright. What I'm getting at is that being a Christian isn't just about believing or taking part in the church's sacraments; it's about becoming, in actual practice, a new sort of person.

THE GOOD LIFE

We are turning our attention now to a part of the theological conversation called ethics, or more specifically, **theological ethics**. The term *moral theology* means the same thing. This part of the conversation is simply about how we discern right from wrong and good from bad. One of the things I appreciated about teaching undergraduates was honesty—not mine necessarily, but theirs. I don't mean that there weren't the usual plagiarism issues and questionable explanations for late work. Those things happened, but there was also a lot of honest conversation about the big issues of that stage of life—questions about work and further education, about sexuality and marriage. One of the underlying questions for some of these students was whether God had a specific and detailed plan for each of their lives. Like most emerging adults, the students I taught were enjoying a new level of freedom. Many were out of their parents' houses for the first time. On their best days, this freedom sparked an eager engagement with fundamental ethical questions: What makes something right? How dependent is the right course of action on the circumstances? Or even more broadly, what is the good life? On their worst days, it meant dumb decisions.

If I stretch things a bit, I could say that my students were acting out some of the classical approaches to the good life. There were the stoics, who believed one should be indifferent to pleasure and pain. There were cynics, who thought the best way forward was to live in continuity with nature, keeping one's wants to a minimum and needing only the bare necessities. The skeptics sought the good life by doubting what others claimed to know. Finally, there were the epicureans, who believed that the good life was found in pleasure and thus sought simple lives without pain or fear. Scholars see traces of each in the New Testament, so it's no surprise that modern Christians are drawn to versions of these approaches too.

There was a time when theologians and philosophers tried to depict the well-lived life as a whole. They linked beauty, truth, and goodness in grand descriptions of what it meant to be human. Now, however, when theologians and philosophers talk about ethical matters, they are prone to focus on specific decisions. For example, is it right to buy a new pair of jeans when the money could feed someone who is starving? Is there a significant difference between *allowing* someone to die by withholding life support and *causing* them to die by administering morphine?

Most of us have a basic approach to ethics. We might look to lists of commandments and start with those, saying that living well is mostly about obeying certain laws or principles. An approach like this is called **deontology**. Or we might shift things a bit and say that the right thing to do is not necessarily to obey a set of rules but rather to obey the command of God in the moment. In this view, Abraham would have been right to kill his son like a sacrificial lamb purely because it was what God told him to do. Yes, it would have been murder—having broken the law against killing the innocent—but it still would have been the "right" thing. We refer to this as an ethic of **divine command**. Near the beginning of his book on ethics, Dietrich Bonhoeffer said that serious Christian thinking on the subject requires us to give up the obvious questions about being good or doing good. All we can do, he said, is ask what God wants.

Bonhoeffer was trying to plow some hard soil. The culture he was speaking to had pressed ethics into a formal system. Many of the Christians he had in mind would have affirmed the existence of God but wouldn't have believed in God's ongoing personal engagement. You can probably see the positive and negative possibilities of the divine command approach pretty quickly. Positively, it requires us to listen to God closely and to never assume at the outset that we know what God will ask us to do. Negatively, of course, it's hard to provide accountability for others if we can never anticipate what God would want.

An alternative proposal is to say that doing the right thing isn't so much about obeying rules as about calculating the right outcome. We call this **consequentialism**. We sometimes get into this sort of thinking when we use the word *discernment*. We try to discern the right course of action when we don't think it's obvious. Early Christians needed to figure out whether it was all right to eat food sacrificed to idols and how they should support the poor in their midst. The apostles helped discern how this should happen. Finally, there is the perspective that Paul seems to focus on in the passage I referenced in the opening of this chapter, Galatians 5. This is a virtue ethic, or more technically, **aretaicism**. Virtue ethics is concerned with the development of good character.

Think of these perspectives this way: Imagine you're driving a bus full of schoolchildren. They are all above average and immensely talented. As you round a corner high in the mountains (you're taking them on a fancy field trip), a car driven by the current winner of the Nobel Peace Prize stalls sideways in front of you. He never took the time to learn to operate a manual transmission properly. You're going too fast to stop. There are three teachers on the bus. Mr. Deontology yells, "Never kill the innocent. Run the driver over!" Ms. Divine Command wails mournfully, "Lord Jesus, tell our driver what to do." Ms. Consequentialism says: "That Nobel Laureate will save thousands, take us over the cliff!" The last voice you hear—it must be Mr. Aretaicism—says, "You're a good person. We trust your courage and love." You somehow manage to throw *yourself* under the bus and save everyone. Later, while you're recovering in the hospital, you tell a reporter that you didn't actually act out of bravery; you were just confused by the other options. Thankfully, she leaves that out of her article.

There doesn't seem to be any reason to think that we must choose between these various modes of ethical reasoning. They all show up in the Bible. When Jesus, in Matthew 22, is asked about the greatest commandment, he famously replies that it is to love God with our heart, soul, and mind and to love one's neighbor as one's self (see vv. 37 and 39, for example). That's the core of it. That seems to be what Jesus modeled for his followers. How we might do that in any particular situation, though, requires some careful thought. Being able to do that consistently and fully requires God's grace and a lifetime of faithful practice. Faithful practice is how we learn to love the right things.

Each of our lives takes place in the time between the resurrection of Jesus and his return. Another way to describe this period of time is to say it is the time for the church. It is in the Christian community that we learn to speak truthfully and love rightly. It's here that we grow in our call to bear God's image in this good world. It's here that we learn to participate in God's reconciling work. It's here that we learn to be ambassadors of God's peace. This is part of the reason that I often found myself encouraging my students to make participation in the church a foundational commitment. None of us can know what future challenges life will bring our way. Being part of a living community invigorated by God's Spirit means we have a fighting chance at responding like Jesus.

WORK

Most of us will spend much of our lives working: we will study, we will build things, we will care for people or manage a business. For most of human history the sort of work one did was dictated by one's family or gender. One was a shoemaker because one's father was a shoemaker. A woman would stay home and care for a household because, well, she was a woman. While this remains true for some people today, it isn't as overwhelming as it once was. Most people now have at least enough leisure and income to go to school for a while. That's a way of gaining freedom. This is obviously quite wonderful. Just because your mom worked the farm doesn't mean you must. Of course, this now means that you have to *decide* what to do. This takes us into territory unfamiliar to most biblical characters. The ancient Israelites were not prone to sitting under trees and wondering what they ought to do with their lives. For them it was usually obvious.

The term that often gets used in this conversation is **vocation**. It comes from Latin and implies being called or summoned. In the Catholic world someone with a vocation is someone called to be a priest or a monk. Protestants have been more inclined to speak of normal jobs as vocations. Part of the rationale is that we don't want to split the world into a sacred sphere and a secular sphere, where the former is closer to God and more holy than the latter. However, this is a hard distinction to shake. Many Christian kids grow up with the sense that the people who are really serious about their faith become preachers or youth pastors.

It is not at all obvious from Scripture that God calls everyone to some specific line of work. Paul uses the word *call* several times in the first chapter of his letter to the church in Corinth. He references his own call as an apostle, but when he's speaking about the call of his audience, it is simply a call to the "fellowship" of Jesus Christ. What is our calling? It's simple—follow Jesus. Our vocation is just to be Christians, to grow into the form of Christ. In that we become fully human.

Work remains valuable for Christians, however, because it's an important part of being human. In 2 Thessalonians 3, Paul warns against idleness and commends working to support oneself. Yet there are people who do no appreciable work—the very ill, the very young, even the very old—and surely this does not detract from their humanity. There's little biblical evidence to suggest that a young person or someone at a career junction ought to wait around for some sense of divine call to a specific line of work. That said, there certainly are forms of work that don't fit at all with the Christian faith. Some work contributes directly to human suffering, and some involves deep compromises of basic Christian virtues. When we find ourselves needing to jump through all kinds of hoops to rationalize why we build weapons or create advertising campaigns that are untruthful or sell products by leveraging people's jealousy—it's probably time to look for something that fits better with shalom.

For most of God's people for most of the time, finding a career didn't involve a divine call. It did for some called to be prophets or apostles, but not for most. If we think back to the Torah, being a part of God's people mostly meant things like worshiping God alone, being in right relationship with neighbors, being satisfied with our own possessions, observing a day of rest to signal our trust in God's provision, not being drawn into evil practices by a surrounding culture, teaching children the ways of God, not creating an individualized faith, giving a tithe of our best, periodically canceling debts to preserve the dignity of the poor, and upholding a just system of exchanging goods and settling disputes. This is the sort of stuff that helped communities in the ancient world honor the image of God in each person. It still is. Our work matters, yes, but there's nothing second-rate about simply being called to follow Jesus.

MARRIAGE, SEX, SINGLENESS

When I was in high school there was a couple a few grades ahead of me whom everyone admired. They seemed to fit so well together—as much as seventeen-year-olds can—and they were obviously deeply in love. The rumor was they planned to get married after they graduated, enjoy a shared sex life for a few years, then live together as celibates for the rest of their days. I suppose they were more poetic than the rest of us, or more avant-garde or something, but nobody could figure out why they would make that their goal. Maybe we were just baffled that these people had found someone who would commit to having sex with them for several years. That was beyond the horizon of opportunity for most of us.

Thinking back on that now, I wonder if this couple didn't have a saner view of sex than most of their classmates. Their plan—I have no idea if they followed through—is something of a symbol of the Christian wisdom on sex: it's a good thing, it should be enjoyed, but it isn't the entirety of life. After all, being sexual creatures is about much more than "having sex." It means we enjoy intimacy and touch. It means we are attracted to beauty. We crave things. We want to be known and to know others, and not just in the biblical sense (take a look at the King James Version). Our sexuality and spirituality are not as distinct as we sometimes think.

New Testament Christians believed that "having sex" was not critical to being fully alive. In fact, in 1 Corinthians 7, Paul says that singleness is preferable to marriage. In the first century this was pretty revolutionary, especially in Jewish circles. What early

Christians recognized, though, was that neither marriage nor sexual procreation was necessary for making more Christians. That happened through baptism. Remaining single and celibate has allowed many people the opportunity to serve Christ's mission in profoundly inspiring ways. Given the biblical commendation of singleness, it's surprising how many churches marginalize single people. People whose family status or sexual identity doesn't fit the dominant mold are gifts to be received with gratitude, not problems to be accommodated.

But Paul also writes, "It is better to marry than to be aflame with passion" (1 Corinthians 7:9). Paul's words layer on top of the recognition in Genesis 2 that it isn't good for a person to be alone, and the directive in Genesis 1 to be fruitful. The broad Christian consensus is that sexual intimacy is best experienced within a covenant relationship. God's covenant relationship with humanity is analogous to the covenant of marriage. That theme runs prominently through the Prophets and surfaces again in the New Testament when writers describe Jesus as the groom and God's people as a bride. Aside from serving as an icon for God's relationship with humanity, marriage provides a context for sexual intimacy. As the theologian Stanley Hauerwas writes, "At least one reason for sex being limited to marriage . . . is that marriage provides the context for us to have sex, with its often compromising personal conditions, with the confidence that what the other knows about us will not be used to hurt us. For never are we more vulnerable than when we are naked and making the clumsy gestures necessary to 'make love.'"[2]

Christians have generally said that sex serves three ends: procreation, unification, and pleasure. The first two are long-standing Christian affirmations, the last somewhat less traditional but surely not unbiblical. In Song of Solomon, the lovers are encouraged, "Eat, friends, drink, and be drunk with love" (Song of Solomon 5:1). Surely the God who takes pleasure in creation has nothing against pleasure itself. This threefold way of describing the purpose of sex can help us think through some of the challenging questions related to stewarding our sexuality.

As much as any other part of our lives, our sexual selves are prodded by two persistent contemporary impulses: **romanticism** and **realism**. Neither is quite what it seems. The logic of the so-called realist, in sexuality and in other moral arenas, is that the way things are is the way they should be. Christians are wary of any sort of realism that doesn't take Jesus into account, for in Jesus we see what is ultimately realistic. Just as Jesus shows us that loving one's enemy is realistic and that death's power is ultimately hollow, so he shows us that we need not be ruled by our every desire.

Where the realist says that marital vows are made to be broken, the romantic says that our sexual lives are all about self-realization or emotional fulfillment. The romantic says that life doesn't really begin until we have found "the one" or until we have become sexually active. Again, Jesus shows us otherwise. He shows us that love takes work and that it is sometimes difficult. Just as there are "realists" within the Christian community, so there are "romantics." In addition to embracing the standard-issue romantic notions, some Christians are so keen to emphasize the goodness of sexual intimacy within the bounds of a covenant relationship that they obsess about a person's past, making virginity seem more important than ongoing faithfulness. Or they give the impression that Christian marriages are nothing but bliss. Both of these are unhelpful.

Oriented toward unification, procreation, and pleasure, sexual intimacy affirms that children are the fruit of their parents' love, their desire for each other, and their shared commitment. This is not to say that every child beloved of God is conceived on these terms or to say that sex which cannot lead to offspring is necessarily inappropriate. It is to say, however, that from a

Christian perspective, the love that accompanies sexual intimacy ought to be other-oriented and enacted in thankfulness for the gifts God gives us. Framed by this covenantal context, sex—like worship, like acts of service, like prayer—traces the basic shape of the Christian life. The openness to children that regularly accompanies sexual intimacy, though it need not always do so, demonstrates the hope we have that the world's future will not be as appalling as it may appear. Sex is part of the glue that binds spouses together in the sort of long-term relationship that allows for our growth into the image of God in flesh.

The key to actually doing the whole Christian life thing—ethical conundrums included—is the church. The church is not just a place for expressing our good ideas about God or waving our hands in starry-eyed wonder. The church is a place where we learn how to live well. It should be a place where we all—regardless of whether we are bound by marital vows, whether we are parents, whether we are on a great career path—can apprentice in the way of Jesus.

Learning how to live life well often involves following someone who follows Jesus. Paul says as much in the eleventh chapter of his first letter to the Corinthians. The Christian community provides us with these examples—if not in our immediate context, then in the lives of the saints. When we find ourselves in conversation with them—reading what they've written or learning about their lives—we would be best served by listening. They knew that we all live in a time when creation, though it remains good and beautiful, groans for the completion of its renewal in Christ. They knew that we live in a time when each culture contains wonderful things worth celebrating and terrible things worth bringing to a halt. To navigate such crosscurrents requires great skill and sturdy character. It requires honest companions, dead and alive. It requires those who remind us that we are loved by God and called to follow the one in whom the fullness of God dwelt.

17

I SAW *a* NEW HEAVEN *and a* NEW EARTH

Hope

Hope, in a Christian sense, is love stretching itself into the future.
—**Miroslav Volf**

We live in an age suspicious of hope. This is partly because hope is often used to sell things or to get us to buy into someone's political agenda. We know enough history to know that some things that seemed like great achievements at the time have ended in disasters. On the more tedious end of the scale is what we're learning about the fleece jackets some of us wear to stay warm when we hike. Apparently when we wash these things, they shed small plastic fibers that go right through the filters of washing machines and sewage plants, ending up in the ocean and

in the food chain. On the more dramatic end of the scale is our
ability to split the atom.

Jürgen Moltmann was born in Hamburg, Germany in 1926.
He fought in World War II and spent several years as a prisoner
of war. He began reading the Bible in that context and became
a Christian. Moltmann returned home after the war to find his
homeland in ruins. His theological writing has chased hope ever
since. How do we find hope in an age characterized by misuse
of power? Moltmann writes that the foundation for Christian
hope is found not in "the ups and down of the moods of the time,
but in the promise of the coming God."[1] The Bible is laced with
hope. In fact, we can say that as much as a Christian community
is known by the beliefs and lives of its members, it is also known
by their hope.

One of my favorite memories of living in Western Canada was
the time I spent a December evening at an outdoor Christmas
pageant. We sat on wooden bleachers in a farmyard. The audio
portion of the show was a recording played through loudspeak-
ers. A guy named Mark would press *pause* on the recording while
the actors prepared for a new scene, then press *play* again when
everyone was lined up and ready. The shepherds spent most of the
night circled around a fire in a barrel. When they had to herd the
sheep away from the warmth, some of them lit cigarettes.

But the highlight for me was the moment when the angel
stepped atop the hay bale, raised a pretend trumpet to his lips—
and nothing happened. He looked up at the stars for a moment,
then raised the trumpet again. Still nothing. Then the angel
stepped off his haybale perch and—I was just close enough to
hear—said, "Mark, what *on earth* are you doing?" (Actually, he
had not lived into his angelic character sufficiently to say "on
earth.") Turns out Mark had gotten lost in the script.

I almost didn't go that night, it was so cold. But that moment,
with the farmer-angel putting the trumpet to his lips and waiting

in the cold for sound to come out of the speaker wired to a farm-yard pole—well, that was worth it.

Much of knowing what we are to do depends on knowing where we are in the story. This means it's critical that we know what God has done and what God will do. The final book of the Bible is the book of Revelation. No other book in the canon, except maybe Genesis, has spawned so much disagreement or so many bad movies. The book of Revelation, also called the Apoc-alypse of John, is full of comic-book-like images: a beast with seven heads, a red dragon, a white horse. In Revelation, govern-ments are personified and economic systems are boiled down to a symbol. We've talked about the book of Daniel already and the smaller apocalyptic chunks in Matthew 24 and 25, but the book of Revelation is the most famous chunk of apocalyptic literature in the Bible.

I've always felt that my experience in the farmyard on that December night was a bit apocalyptic, in the sense of disclosing some reality or knowledge. That pageant showed me what the church is like. It's a drama troop with hardly any training trying to present the story of God coming into our world. Sometimes we try too hard, and we often do a clumsy job. Sometimes we get frustrated with each other before a watching world. At times we miss our cues. If those watching us are gracious, they realize how awfully cold it is.

The book of Revelation is about the cold. It is about worship and about the triumph of a slaughtered Lamb. At the beginning of the book is a series of messages to seven area churches. This sets the book both in a specific situation, since these churches were real communities, and in the universal situation, since the number seven signifies completeness and entirety. Then, in chapter 4, the book describes the throne room of the Master of the universe. John weeps at the sight of it because nobody—none of the heav-enly creatures, none of the elders—can open the scroll held in the

Master's hand. None, that is, except a Lamb that looked "as if it had been slaughtered" (Revelation 5:6). At the core of things, the comic-book vision seems to say, We do not find the sort of power we would expect. There's no huge dude with a sword, no glowing orb of nuclear force. There's just this Lamb. Lambs are not fierce at all. I once found one that had drowned in a bucket. John's Lamb is an icon of sacrificial innocence and—here's the surprising turn—of divine power. God's power is anything but what we expect.

The Lamb opens the scroll, and what follows is a series of overlapping images: seven seals, seven lampstands, seven trumpets, seven angels, and so on. This cascade of pictures tells the story of imperial power and the persecution of God's people. We readers are pulled through these images to the scene of judgment. The prophets might have called it the day of the LORD. It's the time when evil will finally be put into its place and even death will be carted away. John's great vision into the heart of things wraps up with a picture of renewal. There's no good way to summarize it; we must let John speak for himself:

> Then I saw a new heaven and a new earth. . . . And I saw the holy city, the new Jerusalem, coming down out of heaven from God, prepared as a bride adorned for her husband. And I heard a loud voice from the throne saying,
>
> > "See, the home of God is among mortals.
> > He will dwell with them;
> > they will be his peoples,
> > and God himself will be with them;
> > he will wipe every tear from their eyes.
> > Death will be no more;
> > mourning and crying and pain will be no more,
> > for the first things have passed away."
>
> And the one who was seated on the throne said, "See, I am making all things new." (Revelation 21:1-5)

Notice that John says making *all things* new, not making *all new* things. I forget where I first heard that distinction, but it's a critical one. The book of Revelation is about the redemption of things that already exist. It's the warmth of the approaching spring.

The terrible images wrapped up in the book of Revelation remind us that the full consummation of God's redemptive work has yet to take place. We're a bit like people on our way back to shore after being rescued from a life raft adrift for weeks at sea. There was a moment when we *were* saved. Yet we *are* still being saved. And truthfully, too, we *will be* saved yet more fully than we are now. Being picked up out of our raft and being motored back to shore are both critical operations. But the rescue isn't complete until we've made it back to a place where we can grow potatoes and pet the dog. We need to get back to land. We sometimes refer to this past-present-future unfolding of salvation as justification, sanctification, and glorification. Justification is about receiving good standing with God. Sanctification is about growing into the form of Jesus. Glorification is about seeing God clearly and finally being cut free from the weight of suffering.

The early Christians expected the return of Jesus to complete this work, to move them from a three-tensed salvation to a place where it was all in the past. To the surprise of some, this did not happen during their lifetime. We refer to this delay of Jesus' return as the delay of the **Parousia**. Because things didn't wrap up as quickly as some of the early Christian communities anticipated, there were those who poked fun. The author of 2 Peter calls these critics "scoffers" and describes how they took this lack of action as license to live as though God was not the Lord of the universe. He reminds these Christians of what the psalmist says in the ninetieth chapter: that a day on God's calendar is like a thousand years on ours. Waiting for the completion of things isn't a matter of watching the calendar or adding up days and trying to figure out some cryptic code in the Bible. I can think of at least three or four prominent predictions of Christ's return in my life alone. They were all wrong.

A skeptical preacher once pointed out that Jesus says that nobody knows the day or the hour, not even the angels (Matthew 24:36). If that's true, this preacher observed, then anytime someone predicts a specific time, all we know is that it won't be that time. As it is, our lives—the lives of shopkeepers and the lives of dictators—are all encased in the patience of God.

I remember a time traveling abroad with a group of Americans. We were walking down the street when a shopkeeper came rushing out to us. He held a newspaper out toward us and adamantly asked, "Is this your justice? Is this your freedom?" It was a lament more than a confrontation. I went over to see the paper he held out. The front page was covered with pictures of living, naked bodies piled in front of leering soldiers in a prison in Iraq. That shopkeeper waits for justice. The detainees who were mocked wait for justice. The soldiers, in over their heads, also wait for justice. And none of them merely want one nation's warped sense of justice. They all want true, divine justice. We know what we have isn't that. So we wait, and with the psalmist we wonder, "How long, O Lord?" (Psalm 13:1).

The basic setup of our waiting is simply this: we live in a time between the times. Or we might say we live in a period of overlapping eons. The new age began with the resurrection of Jesus, and because of that, we can see the approaching end of the old age. Through the power of the Spirit, Jesus has brought to an end the ambitions of sin and death. They know, and we know, that they will not triumph. Yet we know too that they have not yet been entirely rounded up—war, death, and imprisonment are evidence of that. One day, though, that will come to an end. The old age will discontinue, leaving only the new.

Christians haven't always been willing to speak of this era as simply as that—as a time between the times. And so we've come up with ways to parse things more distinctly. In the late nineteenth century, some prominent Protestants spoke a lot about "dispensations" of history, or distinct periods in which God ruled in a particular way. There was the dispensation of innocence before sin; the dispensation of the patriarchs; the dispensation under the Law of Moses; the current dispensation of grace in the age of the church; and so on. This mechanical approach to history has been unimaginatively named **dispensationalism**. Dispensationalism is rooted in a group known as the Plymouth Brethren, named after the English town where they held meetings. John Nelson Darby, D. L. Moody, and C. I. Scofield were all influential dispensationalist voices. This approach has spread widely through the Scofield Reference Bible. It's a version of the Bible that includes dispensationalist commentary. The whole church agrees that there are developments in the story of redemption, but dispensationalism itself has remained a (powerful) fringe view.

Some contemporary scholars, like N. T. Wright and Kevin Vanhoozer, have begun speaking of salvation history as a multi-act play: act 1 is creation, act 2 is the fall, and so on through Israel, Jesus, the church, and the final act, which is Jesus' return and the renewal of creation. For these scholars, the point isn't so much to divvy history up just right as it is to suggest that living the Christian life is like theatrical improvisation. We know the first series of acts, and we know how our act has begun, but it falls to us to carry on the drama. In improv, you don't have a script to work with—just other actors and the story that precedes your arrival on the scene.

The kingdom of God is here but not fully. It is "already but not yet." This last phrase is one that's used a lot in this part of the conversation. It's an attempt at speaking to the fact that the kingdom of God is here *already* but *not yet* here in fullness. Jesus is king, but is not universally recognized. This makes for an adventurous situation. It calls for creativity as we remember and extend the story. Our confidence in God's love and authority gives us freedom to experiment and to take risks. However, our place in the drama can also be intimidating: nothing is lined out for us.

We expect that there will be ways in which we don't fit with societies run by doomed powers. Many of God's children have felt as though they've been chased by a dragon or trounced by a multiheaded monster. Whether that's our experience or not, we should remember that God has given us two key resources. One is the presence of God's Spirit. We are never alone. In John 14, Jesus describes the Spirit as the Advocate, or the Helper. This is no small gesture. It isn't lip service. Our Helper is the same Spirit that resurrected Jesus from the dead. We also have been given the Christian community. This is a real body, brought to life by the Spirit. It's a faulted and sinful body, yes. But through its speech, through its hands and feet, the good news of Jesus continues to reshape our world.

ZOOMING IN

What we've discussed above can all be lumped under the heading of **general eschatology**. That's the big-picture stuff. But we probably have more particular questions. What about us or what about our loved ones? What about heaven and hell? When we ask those kinds of questions, we're beginning to talk about **personal eschatology**. When we move to this part of the discussion in the classroom or the parish hall, I try to always remind the group that we need to be careful. We're working with metaphors and vague statements. We should be mindful that over the centuries Christians have used this stuff in manipulative ways. We've used it like the story of Santa: lump of coal if you're bad, gift certificate to the mall if you're good. We might be tempted to think that we can figure out the final destiny of individuals. We should never go there. It's God's judgment that matters, not ours.

As much as it's generally a good idea for us to not say too much about these issues, as a pastor I have realized that people do want some idea of what it is that Christians generally believe. So here it is: When it comes to life beyond death, Christian communities have generally affirmed two events and two states. We expect a bodily resurrection—an event. In 1 Corinthians, Paul lays out how central the resurrection of Jesus is for the entire faith. It's central to what we believe about Jesus, but it's also central to what we hope for in the future. Paul describes Jesus as "the first fruits of those who have died" (1 Corinthians 15:20).

The life to come is not exactly like the one we know now. Paul is aware of that. In Matthew 22, Jesus says there will be no marriage in the next life. So things will be different. Back in 1 Corinthians, Paul turns to an agricultural metaphor to speak about the resurrection. Our present bodies are like dry seeds. Our new ones will be far superior to them, like spiritual bodies compared to earthly ones. There will be bodies, though—let's not miss that. We don't expect the dead to become disembodied sparks or stars. Chubby angel bodies—maybe. Romance novel cover bodies—we just don't know. There will be bodies, though, and Paul says they will be imperishable.

The second event that Christians generally affirm is judgment. This is the identification of the righteous and unrighteous. I don't know if you've ever been in a class with a real keener—someone who thought they knew what the teacher wanted and thought they would get it just right. What Scripture does—I'm thinking of Matthew 24 and 25 here—is overturn any keener-type notions we might have about judgment. When Jesus speaks of the separation of the sheep and the goats, both herds are surprised. However, the very existence of judgment is one of the more controversial aspects of the faith.

Theology conferences are events that only a few people really enjoy. I'm one of those few people. I love these things. I was at a conference once where a theology student from the Netherlands presented a paper that suggested we should stop thinking about judgment. He said it wasn't a core part of the faith—that judgment just didn't fit with the love displayed through the life of Jesus. We should just get it out of our heads. After his presentation, a peace worker from the Philippians, a guy with a ponytail, said something like, "I work with poor people. These people, and their families before them, have been taken advantage of by the rich for generations." Those of us in the conference room began to squirm a bit. The ponytailed peace guy continued: "There is no way for the people I work with to ever get themselves out of poverty. My mission organization helps a bit, but we can't really do much. Wealthy families control the government and prevent reform. I understand why average people want to pick up a gun. I wouldn't, but I understand why others do." The room was quiet. He concluded, "I don't know what things are like in your country, but in my country we need God's judgment. Poor people want God to do something, because nobody else can." The exchange was emblematic. Those who have experienced injustice, not just hurt feelings, know that what we need is a just judge.

In addition to these two events, we also anticipate two eternal states: we've traditionally referred to these as heaven and hell. I'm not sure these terms are the most helpful. Scripture seems to suggest that rather than heaven, the future destiny of the blessed is a new creation. Think of Revelation 21: a renewed earth fits with the bodily resurrection we just spoke about. A renewed earth and a bodily resurrection uphold the beauty and goodness of skin, bones, and dirt. The term *heaven* is used in two ways throughout the Bible: in the plural (the heavens) to speak of the sky, and in the singular to speak of the dwelling place of God within creation. Thus Jesus teaches us to pray that God's will be done on earth as it already is in heaven. Heaven is not the eternal dwelling place of the righteous. Not every biblical reference to heaven lines up exactly like this, but it's pretty close.

The term *hell* is similarly troubled. Contemporary Christians tend to use it too easily, and more directly than Scripture itself does. Multiple biblical terms are sometimes rendered as "hell." In the Old Testament there is Sheol, the dwelling place of the dead. In the New Testament there is Gehenna, which seems to be a metaphorical reference to a burning garbage dump near Jerusalem. And there is also hades, a term for the underworld adopted from other ancient Near Eastern cultures. Some readers of Scripture have synthesized these references and found them to point more or less to our commonly held picture of hell as a place of eternal conscious torment. Much of this is drawn from places in the Gospels where Jesus speaks of an eternal or unquenchable fire.

We discussed already the universalist approach to things, which says that if something like hell exists, it will ultimately be unpopulated. Others think the reference to "hell" throughout the Bible can be best understood as a description of destruction. This view is sometimes described as **contingent immortality**. It emphasizes the idea that if we choose to disconnect ourselves from the source of life, we will simply cease to be. It's hard not to speculate too much here. The Bible's images are ripe for the picking, and when it comes to these topics, we often find ourselves quite hungry.

SEEING THROUGH A GLASS DARKLY

My son picked up a seashell. The shard drew our attention because of its vivid coloring, blue and yellow slashed with black ribs against a calcareous white field. We passed it back and forth. He stood on the beach in rubber boots, I squatted beside him in yellow sandals. The two of us were drawn to that small thing, even though the leftovers of waves played around our feet and the largest ocean in the world, the Pacific, churned at our backs.

There is beauty and drama in the vastness of the ocean, but my son and I watched the shifting sunlight change the coloring of the small thing we held. We marveled, even, at its texture.

Somehow or other, most of us have clung to the truism that all good things must come to an end. My college teaching appointment lasted about eight years, and I loved it. In the seventh year, the institution's board decided to rethink the theological tenets that guided the school. I had hoped they would open things up to welcome a wider swath of the Christian community. Like so many theological schools in post-Christendom countries, ours was in trouble. Shrinking churches meant a shrinking enrollment. To clarify its niche, the college latched on to one of the issues North American evangelicals thought so important in those days: the historicity of Adam and Eve. The institution's leaders thought it was critical that faculty teach with confidence that these biblical figures were real, historical people. At one point the provost came in to my office, sat down, and asked me if I could affirm this. "I don't think so," I said. "I'm not sure one way or the other. I doubt it, though, and I don't think it's a critical issue." Suddenly I was the odd one out and my teaching tenure was over. It was a small town. Everyone knew.

The school gave my family and me a year to find something new. We would spend part of that year near the Benedictine monastery, praying about what was next. I stood on the beach with my son only a week after being told that I wasn't welcome to keep teaching. I had not yet told my son that we would have to move. There was too much beauty there for that kind of news.

Someday, when he is older, I will tell him the whole story. I will tell him, too, that truth and mystery are swirled together. I will tell him that we can't speak of one without the other. I will say that theology is about what we believe, but also what we doubt. Faith, as I see it, implies doubt. It's holding something to be true when we know we could be wrong. Faith is living into a view of the world tinted by Paul's darkened glass. That is how it is. There is no other way. For now.

In Revelation 22, John tells us that an angel gave him a tour of the New Jerusalem. The city had symbolically descended to earth, yet John relays his experience with anticipation of a real future. The throne of God and the Lamb will be there. God's servants from all nations will see their Creator face-to-face, and there will be no more night. John says, "They [will] need no light of lamp or sun, for the Lord God will be their light, and they will reign forever and ever" (v. 5). I suspect that all words of theology will be turned into words of worship. We will no longer need to speak tentatively of God. We will need no more guides. God will be right there.

18

The TASK *of* THEOLOGY

Let me seek you in desiring you; let me desire you in seeking you. Let me find you in loving you; let me love you in finding you.
—**Anselm of Canterbury**

Having good conversations about God is not easy for many of us. In his book *The Shallows*, technology writer Nicholas Carr argues that the massive amount of time many of us spend on the Internet is changing the way we think. He says, "The Net delivers precisely the kind of sensory and cognitive stimuli—repetitive, intensive, interactive, addictive—that have been shown to result in strong and rapid alterations in brain circuits and functions." The ability to skim and skitter through dozens of websites has certain advantages, but it comes at the cost of being able to concentrate and think deeply. Carr puts it provocatively: "If, knowing what we know today about the brain's plasticity, you were to set out to invent a medium that would rewire our mental circuits as quickly and thoroughly as possible, you would probably end up designing something that looks and works a lot like the Internet."[1]

In writing this book, I've become convinced that the research Carr has in mind applies to me. Far too many breaks to check the news, MLB box scores, or even just my email have made this project take longer than it should have. This inability to dig deep and concentrate is only one of the challenges our contemporary Christian communities face. I can't help but wonder what it would be like if we were able to sit down and talk together about all we've covered over the last seventeen chapters. I imagine that some of you might want to talk a bit more about theology, not so much about the biblical content as about the *how* of it. This sort of a question has us circling back to some fundamental questions about theology: What is it? How do we do it? Does it matter?

A modern-day Catholic theologian has said that a theologian "is someone who watches their language in the presence of God."[2] I like that way of putting it, especially as it applies to the on-again, off-again theological work we all do. This means that speaking theologically isn't just something we work on by learning vocabulary and historical chronology; theology is also something that works on us. This is one of the reasons that the contemporary loss of spiritual and theological language is so concerning. Many of us have absorbed a lot of lies about God and ourselves, about our neighbors and the world. Watching our language in the presence of God can change that.

For ancient philosophers like Plato and Aristotle, theology meant scrutinizing the poetic myths about the Greek pantheon. They weren't fond of theology. For Augustine, theology was the "study of the divine nature."[3] He extended the implications of that study into politics and many other things. For the English theologian Richard Hooker, theology was "the science of things divine."[4] Calling theology a "science" is an allusion to the fact that it has a regular set of sources and methods. Each of these definitions is true as far as the etymology of the word goes. But we probably sense that there's more to theology than this.

Anselm of Canterbury famously described theological work as "faith seeking understanding." This doesn't fully describe theology, but it does suggest something important. Anselm draws our attention to how part of what we are doing when we have really good theological conversations is reflecting on an acknowledgment of God that already exists in our hearts. The acknowledgment comes first, then the careful examination and explanation. This way of putting it reminds us that the study of theology isn't something we do objectively, like investigating a lab specimen. Truthful speech is something we live.

SPEAKING WITH THE SAINTS

To fill out the understanding of theology that we've been developing throughout this book, it might help to compare it to two other types of study. First, there is the academic discipline of **religious studies**. Scholars working in the field of religious studies analyze the history and variety of various forms of religious expression. They try to explain key texts, practices, and beliefs. This sort of inquiry doesn't assume any faith commitment on the part of the scholar—at least nothing except a general assumption that religion can be studied using academic tools. A second related field is **biblical studies**. Scholars working in this field analyze the origin, development, literary features, and so on, of specific texts. Again, no particular faith commitment is necessary. Neither scholars in religious studies nor scholars in biblical studies make explicit claims about how things should be or who God is. They are more interested in explaining who some other group thinks God is and how a particular set of beliefs developed over time. There's value in those approaches.

But theology is different. When we are speaking as theologians, we are making claims about how God should be understood and what we should do in response. This might seem arrogant, but in reality, we all hold beliefs about God and we all hold beliefs about how people should live. That's true even if we think that no one should force their beliefs on anyone else. Any opinion about what others should do is a belief held with **normative intent**. We all think our beliefs are true. Vocational theologians are a bit like some philosophers in this way: both make claims about the nature of reality and how we know it. Unlike the field of philosophy, however, theology means working within the constraints of traditional sources. For Christians, as with Muslims, Jews, and others, the most obvious source is a text. Adherents of all religious traditions theologize in one way or another. This conversation is where most of the world's inhabitants engage the big questions of life. This is why theology has been, and should continue to be, an important part of public and academic life.

An important word here is **doctrine**. This term simply refers to what Christian communities teach to be true and what shapes their lives. More specifically, doctrine is a carefully formulated set of claims about belief and practice. Doctrine seems like a dated term—maybe even an outdated one—because it isn't used much in modern translations of the Bible. In older translations, the King James Version for example, the Greek words *didachē* and *didaskalia* were often translated into English as "doctrine." In some modern translations, the word is simply translated as "teaching." Theology is the reflective practice of developing and applying doctrine. Relating our changing understanding of a text to an ever-changing context means that elements of doctrine change too. The key is that doctrine is a carefully formulated set of claims about belief and practice—it's not just gut-response application.

"That is all still a bit murky," you might say. "It doesn't really get at the question of how we do theology." Well, the *how* is what I've been trying to show throughout this book. We've been reading the biblical text in the context of our lived experience; we've been doing this under the guidance of the Christian community's tradition; and we've been doing this with the tools of reason in hand. That's clunkier than Anselm's line—faith seeking understanding—but it's the best way I can put it.

Stating it this way, though, highlights the sources we draw on when we do theology: Scripture, experience, tradition, and reason. These are the four legs that hold up the theological stool. These sources are sometimes referred to as the **Wesleyan quadrilateral**. John Wesley was never so specific about this, but the term has stuck anyway.

Some Protestants are particularly leery of speaking about tradition. They have a hard time seeing the need for this leg of the stool. With what we've said about the Reformation, you probably know why. There was a time when tradition was overemphasized, when its value trumped that of the Bible. We might be able to redeem tradition a bit, though, by remembering that the Christian community has been reading Scripture for nearly two millennia. The Spirit has been at work in this community the whole way along. Why not pay attention to how the Spirit has led the church in the past? It's not that we can't make some new choices. Repentance and changing direction is a thing Christians do. However, we should still let the ancients speak.

Another way to think about this is to say that theological conversation is a conversation with the dead. That might sound strange—as if we channel spirits or have coffee with vampires. But what I'm talking about is the assumption that the barrier between the dead and the living is permeable. This is because we believe in the **communion of saints**. One of the places we encounter this idea in the Bible is in Hebrews 11 and 12. The basic point is that the Christian community includes a "cloud of witnesses," those who have gone before. G. K. Chesterton (1874–1936) describes this aspect of theology with his characteristic sauciness:

> Tradition means giving votes to the most obscure of all classes, our ancestors. It is democracy of the dead. Tradition refuses to submit to the small and arrogant oligarchy of those who merely happen to be walking about. All democrats object to men being disqualified by the accident of birth; tradition objects to them being disqualified by the accident of death.[5]

The point is that when it comes to God, we must avoid the assumption that only now, finally, in our own time, have we gotten it right. The community that reads Scripture and allows it to shape their lives reaches deep into the past and—though we often forget this—into the future. By thinking of those who will come after us, we are reminded that they will have to correct for our mistakes. The dead in every era made errors, and so do we. It is this conviction that opens up the theological conversation to revision and change. This means our goal is never to reach an end point where everything is finally clear and right. Our goal is humble faithfulness in our time.

If tradition makes its way into the conversation through our acknowledgment of the Spirit's work in the past and the communion of saints, what do we make of the rest of the quadrilateral? We have already discussed Scripture at some length, but we have not said much about experience or reason. Looking to our personal experience to garner information about God is tricky. We each have a propensity to be wrong, and we are prone to identify God with all kinds of harmful things. For instance, we might be tempted to say that God has some specific trait identified with our gender, race, or social position. We are tempted to do this because it gives us leverage over others. It's probably better to think of our own experience as the context within which God

speaks. It lets us see new things in Scripture. But if we extend
the idea of experience beyond ourselves—say to the experiences
of those in the global church and to the historical church—then
we have something we can work with. There are others who can
pray with us and, as we read in 1 John 4:1, others who can "test
the spirits" with us. That's valuable.

In the wake of World War II, when Christians around the
world learned the true, horrific extent of the Holocaust, an obvious question came up. The culture that perpetrated the deaths
of some six million Jewish people was ostensibly Christian. It
inhabited land that was once the cradle of the Reformation.
How did this happen? That question has nothing but complicated answers, but one element of it was the anti-Judaism nursed
by Christians for more than a thousand years. In Matthew 27,
Pilate hands Jesus over to the crowd in an attempt to separate
himself from the outcome. The crowd responds, "His blood be
on us and on our children!" (v. 25). For centuries, this text was
the lens through which Christians read other parts of Scripture.
It was only after seeing the horrific consequences of such a hermeneutical approach that the global Christian community made
a wholesale revision. This did not amount to snipping this passage out of the Bible. Instead, it was an acknowledgment that
the larger context of the Bible affirms God's ongoing love for
the Jewish people. It makes anti-Semitism absurd. No major
Christian group that I'm aware of would now say that the line
from Matthew 27 is grounds for treating Jewish people with
anything less than love and the full dignity of those who bear
God's image. In this case, large-scale experience was part of an
important theological shift. The same thing has proven true with
respect to slavery. Slavery was once defended on the basis of a
few lines from Genesis 9 that describe some of Noah's descendants, as well as the fact that the New Testament doesn't offer
explicit condemnation. Yet Christians now acknowledge, based

in large part on the horrors of slavery itself, that the trajectory of Scripture as a whole makes slavery absurd.

What about reason? As you might have surmised from the preceding paragraphs and from our discussion of natural revelation early in the book, reason cannot do much theological work on its own. Yet reason is clearly a tool we use in theological discussion. In fact, there is no part of the conversation in which our rational faculties are not engaged. Forgive me for sounding peevish, but the idea that faith and reason are somehow opposed is silly. We should stop juxtaposing the words as though there might be a way to live with one and not the other. Throughout the history of the church, committed Christians have, for example, been involved in cutting-edge science. Modern genetics began with the work of an Augustinian monk named Gregor Mendel (1822–84), and the theory of the expanding universe was developed by a Belgian priest, Georges Lemaître (1894–1966). I assume most of us know Christians who use reason all the time: auto mechanics, doctors, researchers, computer programmers, farmers.

TRUTH, BEAUTY, AND GOODNESS

Several years after beginning to teach theology, I was invited to become a regular member of the preaching rotation at the Anglican church my family and I attended. It was not a large church—this is the one with the plywood cutouts of the holy family kept in a small shed because there was no room for them in the main building. After every service we made toast and tea, and we talked. For those years it was the right place for my family. We walked there every Sunday, even in the snow. We knew people and they knew us. I gladly prepared sermons once a month. After I got over the initial challenge of speaking to the same group of people over and over again, I found preaching to be a home for my theological vocation in a way I hadn't expected. There's a naturalness to reading and reflecting on Scripture in the context of parish life that one doesn't get in the classroom. So I began to read about pastor-theologians and about the pastoral function of Christian doctrine. Many of the writers I read were the ancients, but I also found a few contemporary writers who were helpful. One of the best was Ellen Charry, a professor of theology at Princeton Theological Seminary.

In 1999, Charry was featured in an article in the American evangelical publication *Christianity Today*. She was described as one of the "new theologians." The author noted that Charry came to faith as an adult, and he wrote, "Charry must be one of the very few persons in all the modern world won to Christ through the reading of theology."[6] She had been a social worker and was searching for a way to put her head and hands together, so she entered graduate studies. One of the theologians she read was Karl Barth. She said, "Barth just undid me. . . . Barth enabled me to first taste that God is a reality and not an idea." Her study of the Augsburg Confession was important too: "Justification by grace through faith . . . what are we talking about? So I decided to try it on. I lifted my arms up and I put it over me like a dress, the doctrine. . . . I tried it. And I fell off the chair. . . . I tried it on like a dress, and I just fell over."[7]

More than most theologians, Charry gets the connections. In her book *By the Renewing of Your Minds*, she observes that ancient Christians believed that "God was the origin and destiny of human happiness, that knowing and loving God are the foundation of human self-knowledge and direction, and that life's goal is conformation to God."[8] Modern Christians have lost these connections; now we have a hard time seeing that what we say theologically can have, as Charry calls it, a "salutary" effect. It can help us flourish. Charry examined some of the most theologically rigorous texts from the Christian tradition, texts like Augustine's *De Trinitate* and Anselm's *Cur Deus homo?* She found that for these older theologians "evangelism, catechesis, moral exhortation, dogmatic exegesis, pastoral care, and apologetics were all happening at the same time because the authors were speaking to a whole person."[9] If something was untrue, they assumed that believing in it would have harmful repercussions. On the other hand, truth, beauty, and goodness affect us positively. This means that the concerns of a pastor for the health of those in her community and the concerns of the theologian for speaking truthfully about God are connected. Getting doctrine right is important, but it is not an end in itself. As I noted earlier, Charry believes that theology "is not just an intellectual art; it cultivates the skill of living well."[10]

Speaking truthfully is not an easy thing. For every idealistic and confident twenty-year-old there is a humble seventy-year-old. Christians have sometimes been too quick and too confident. We have been too quick to name heretics and too quick to say who's outside the camp. Never has this been truer than when self-proclaimed Christians have killed others, including those who bore that same label. Yet we must speak of God—not because of who we are, but because of the character of human life. We cannot make our way without weighing and choosing. We must, in the tradition of the prophets, speak for justice. In addition, as a hopeful people living in a cynical age, we must explain our hope. If we are to serve our communities, we must discover and speak the things we hold to be true. We will recognize our own truthful speech by its hopeful and patient tone. Truth can be spoken patiently. Truth need never be anxious, because it does not need the crutch of violence.

Sometimes it isn't the speaking that is the challenge. In his prison cell, Dietrich Bonhoeffer wrote that there would be times when no words were appropriate, when nothing theological or pious would connect. There are times, as a pastor, when I find that to be true. When members of my congregation are suffering, sometimes nothing can be said. All that we can do is ensure that someone is there, that the body of Christ is present in silent solidarity. There are even times when in our hearts we know the words of our prayers don't really connect us to God. In those times too we fall silent. Our prayers wind their way through zip-lipped pondering. At other times there is conversation. About God. And since God is the source of all that is, we speak about other things too, yes, everything else in the light of God.

Amen.

ACKNOWLEDGMENTS

The rumor is that when Mennonites make a quilt, they deliberately put one stitch in a bit sideways, just so the finished product isn't entirely perfect. I've tried to cover too much in this book for perfection to be my problem. Yet while my name is on the cover, any success this book has achieved is thanks in no small part to the contributions of others.

First, I would like to thank the diverse group of students who heard much of the material presented here in the form of course lectures. Their questions and comments, even their rare bouts with boredom, are the reason the book exists. I'm thankful for the inspiration I received during a short stint as a visiting scholar at Calvin College. It was there that I began working in earnest on this project. I am also thankful to those who read portions of this manuscript, including John Rempel, Lou Bruno, and the group at the Collegeville Institute. Special thanks to David Siegrist for his careful reading of an early draft of the entire manuscript. It has been good to work with the highly skilled folks at Herald Press. Knowing that folks like Valerie Weaver-Zercher and Sara Versluis would help make this book better was one of the reasons I was excited to partner with them.

Finally, saying thanks is not sufficient to acknowledge the joy and inspiration I receive from my wife Sarah and our three little guys at home. Sometimes the best encouragement the four of you offer is simply being interested in other things. Museums, gardening, watching snowplows at three in the morning, art, wrestling, history, home cooking, hikes, a puppy, and staring at the sky— what wonderful stuff to keep me from becoming obsessed with theological inanities.

NOTES

Chapter 1
1. Thomas, *Summa theologica* 1.1.7.
2. Jasper Gerard, "Slow Food Guru Spreads Gospel in High Places," *The Guardian*, June 16, 2007.

Chapter 2
1. As quoted in Thiessen Nation, Siegrist, and Umbel, *Bonhoeffer the Assassin?*, 21 (emphasis added).
2. Seibert, *Violence of Scripture*, 1.
3. Malcolm Gladwell, "Sacred and Profane," *New Yorker*, March 31, 2014.
4. Sanneh, *Whose Religion Is Christianity?*, part 3.
5. Charry, *By the Renewing*, 240.
6. Lamin Sanneh, "Should Christianity Be Missionary? An Appraisal and Agenda," *Dialog* 40, no. 2 (Summer 2001), 87.
7. Billings, *Word of God*, 19.

Chapter 3
1. Alfred Tennyson, "In Memoriam A. H. H.," in *In Memoriam* (Boston: Ticknor, Reed, and Fields, 1850), 86.
2. Wittgenstein, *Philosophical Investigations*, part 2, xi.

3. Chan, *Spiritual Theology*, 45–46.
4. Calvin, *Institutes of the Christian Religion*, 1:43–44.
5. Hart, *Doors of the Sea*, 7–8.
6. Augustine, *Literal Meaning of Genesis*, 42–43.
7. Barth, *Doctrine of Creation* 3.1.81.

Chapter 4

1. Dillard, *Pilgrim at Tinker Creek*, 13–14.
2. Plantinga, *Not the Way*, 14.
3. Gutiérrez, *Theology of Liberation*, 175.
4. Bediako, *Christianity in Africa*, 121.
5. Augustine, *Confessions* 10.40.
6. Augustine, *Treatise against Two Epistles* 4.7.

Chapter 5

1. Julian of Norwich, *Revelations of Divine Love*, 7.
2. As quoted in Carter, *Race*, 228.
3. Gregory of Nyssa, *On the Soul and the Resurrection*, in *Select Writings*, 452.
4. Lausanne Covenant, 1974, available online at http://www.lausanne .org/en/documents/all/26-the-lausanne-covenant.html.
5. Escobar, "Evangelization and Man's Search," 319, 326.
6. Lausanne Covenant.
7. Escobar, *Christian Mission and Social Justice*, 13–15, 74–83.

Chapter 6

1. Bales, *Disposable People*, 6, 9.
2. Ibid., 14–19.
3. Gutiérrez, *Theology of Liberation*, 155.
4. Menno, "Why I Do Not Cease Teaching and Writing," in *Complete Writings*, 398.
5. Gutiérrez, *Theology of Liberation*, ix.
6. Ibid., 35.
7. Cone, *Black Theology of Liberation*, 11.

Chapter 7

1. Ian Brown, "The Magnetic North," *Globe and Mail*, January 17, 2014, https://www.theglobeandmail.com/news/national/the-north/ the-magnetic-north/article16364070/.
2. Berry, *What Are People For?*, 99–100.
3. Boyd, *God of the Possible*, 17.

Chapter 8

1. Augustine, *City of God* 19.7.
2. Trible, *Texts of Terror*, 65.
3. Ibid., 87.

Chapter 9

1. Volf, *A Public Faith*, 57.
2. Ibid., 72–74.

Chapter 10

1. Martin Luther King Jr., "I Have a Dream" (address, 1963 March on Washington for Jobs and Freedom, Washington, DC, August 28, 1963).
2. The Minor Prophets include Hosea, Joel, Amos, Obadiah, Jonah, Micah, Nahum, Habakkuk, Zephaniah, Haggai, Zechariah, and Malachi.
3. Woolman, *Journal of John Woolman*, 30–31.

Chapter 11

1. Kitamori, *Theology of the Pain of God*, 7.
2. Ibid., 45.
3. Ibid., 145.
4. McKnight, *Community Called Atonement*, 107.
5. Bonhoeffer, *Life Together*, 61.

Chapter 12

1. González, *Gospel of Faith and Justice*, 151.
2. Ibid., 153.

Chapter 13

1. Weaver, *Nonviolent Atonement*, 6.
2. Endō, *Silence*, 231.

Chapter 14

1. Coakley, *God, Sexuality, and the Self*, 25. Emphasis removed.
2. Bediako, *Christianity in Africa*, 118. Bediako is reflecting here on the work of John Mbiti.
3. Second Vatican Council, *Lumen Gentium*, November 21, 1964, http://www.vatican.va/archive/hist_councils/ii_vatican_council/documents/vat-ii_const_19641121_lumen-gentium_en.html.

Chapter 15
1. Woodley, *Shalom and the Community*, chap. 3.
2. Smith, *Desiring the Kingdom*, 212.

Chapter 16
1. David Foster Wallace, "This Is Water" (commencement address, Kenyon College, May 21, 2005, Gambier, OH).
2. Hauerwas, "Sex in Public: How Adventurous Christians Are Doing It," in *Hauerwas Reader*, 489.

Chapter 17
1. Moltmann, *Experiment of Hope*, 45.

Chapter 18
1. Carr, *The Shallows*, 116.
2. Nicolas Lash, "Performing Scripture," *Christian Century*, December 11, 2007, 30–35.
3. Augustine, *City of God* 8.1.
4. Hooker, *Laws of Ecclesiastical Polity* 3.8.11.
5. Chesterton, *Heretics/Orthodoxy*, 196.
6. Tim Stafford, "New Theologians," *Christianity Today*, February 8, 1999, 30–49.
7. Quoted in ibid., 47.
8. Charry, *By the Renewing*, 4.
9. Ibid., viii.
10. Ibid., 235, 240.

SELECTED BIBLIOGRAPHY

Augustine. *The City of God against the Pagans*. Edited and translated by R. W. Dyson. Cambridge: Cambridge University Press, 1998.

———. *Confessions*. Translated by Garry Wills. New York: Penguin Classics, 2008.

———. *The Literal Meaning of Genesis*. Translated by J. H. Taylor. New York: Newman Press, 1982.

———. *A Treatise against Two Epistles of the Pelagians*. In *Anti-Pelagian Writings*, trans. Peter Homes and Robert Ernest Wallis and rev. Benjamin B. Warfield. Ser. 1, vol. 5 of *Nicene and Post-Nicene Fathers*, edited by Philip Schaff. Edinburgh: T&T Clark, 1893. http://www.ccel.org/ccel/schaff/npnf105.iii.html.

Bales, Kevin. *Disposable People: New Slaver in the Global Economy*. Berkeley: University of California Press, 2000.

Barth, Karl. *The Doctrine of Creation*. Vol. 3, part 1, of *Church Dogmatics*, edited by G. W. Bromiley and T. F. Torrance. Edinburgh: T&T Clark, 1958. Reprint, Peabody, MA: Hendrickson, 2010.

Bediako, Kwame. *Christianity in Africa: The Renewal of a Non-Western Religion*. Maryknoll, NY: Orbis, 1995.

Berry, Wendell. *What Are People For?* Berkeley: Counterpoint Press, 1990.

Billings, J. Todd. *The Word of God: An Entryway to the Theological Interpretation of Scripture*. Grand Rapids, MI: Eerdmans, 2010.

Bonhoeffer, Dietrich. *Life Together.* Vol. 5 of *Dietrich Bonhoeffer Works,* edited by Geffrey Kelly. Minneapolis: Fortress Press, 1996.

Boyd, Greg. *God of the Possible: A Biblical Introduction to the Open View of God.* Grand Rapids, MI: Baker Academic, 2000.

Calvin, John. *Institutes of the Christian Religion.* 2 vol. Edited by John T. McNeill. Translated by Ford Lewis Battles. Louisville: The Westminster Press, 1960. Reprint, Louisville: Westminster John Knox Press, 2006.

Carr, Nicholas. *The Shallows: What the Internet Is Doing to Our Brains.* New York: Norton, 2012.

Carter, J. Cameron. *Race: A Theological Account.* New York: Oxford University Press, 2008.

Chan, Simon. *Spiritual Theology: A Systematic Study of the Christian Life.* Downers Grove, IL: InterVarsity Press, 1998.

Charry, Ellen. *By the Renewing of Your Minds: The Pastoral Function of Christian Doctrine.* New York: Oxford University Press, 1997.

Chesterton, G. K. *Heretics/Orthodoxy.* Nelson's Royal Classics. New York: Thomas Nelson, 2000.

Coakley, Sarah. *God, Sexuality, and the Self: An Essay "On the Trinity."* Cambridge, UK: Cambridge University Press, 2013.

Cone, James. *A Black Theology of Liberation.* New York: Lippincott, 1970.

Dillard, Annie. *Pilgrim at Tinker Creek.* In *Three by Annie Dillard.* 1974. Reprint, New York: HarperCollins: 2001.

Endō, Shūsaku. *Silence.* Translated by William Johnstone. London: Picador Classic, 1969. Reprint, 2015.

Escobar, Samuel. *Christian Mission and Social Justice.* Scottdale, PA: Herald Press, 1978.

———. "Evangelism and Man's Search for Freedom, Justice and Fulfill-ment." In *Let the Earth Hear His Voice: International Congress on World Evangelization, Lausanne,* Switzerland, edited by J. D. Douglas (Minneapolis: World Wide, 1975), 319–26. Available at https://www.lausanne.org/docs/lau1docs/0309.pdf.

González, Antonio. *The Gospel of Faith and Justice.* Maryknoll, NY: Orbis, 2005.

Gregory of Nyssa. *Select Writings and Letters of Gregory, Bishop of Nyssa.* Translated by William Moore and Henry Austin Wilson. Ser. 2, vol. 5 of *Nicene and Post-Nicene Fathers,* edited by Philip Schaff and Henry Wace. Edinburgh: T&T Clark, 1893.

Gutiérrez, Gustavo. *A Theology of Liberation: History, Politics, and Salvation.* Maryknoll, NY: Orbis, 1973.

Hart, David Bentley. *The Doors of the Sea: Where Was God in the Tsunami?* Grand Rapids, MI: Eerdmans, 2005.

Hauerwas, Stanley. *The Hauerwas Reader.* Edited by John Berkman and Michel Cartwright. Durham, NC: Duke University Press, 2001.

Hooker, Richard. *Of the Laws of Ecclesiastical Polity,* vol 1. Available at http://www.ccel.org/ccel/hooker/reform1.

Julian of Norwich. *Revelations of Divine Love.* Translated by Elizabeth Spearing. New York, Penguin Books, 1998.

Kitamori, Kazoh. *Theology of the Pain of God.* Louisville: John Knox Press, 1965. Reprint, Eugene, OR: Wipf and Stock, 2005.

McKnight, Scot. *A Community Called Atonement.* Nashville: Abingdon, 2007.

Menno Simons. *The Complete Writings of Menno Simons.* Edited by J. C. Wenger. Scottdale, PA: Herald Press, 1984.

Moltmann, Jürgen. *The Experiment of Hope.* Philadelphia: Fortress Press, 1975.

Plantinga, Cornelius, Jr. *Not the Way It's Supposed to Be: A Breviary of Sin.* Grand Rapids, MI: Eerdmans, 1995.

Sanneh, Lamin. *Whose Religion Is Christianity? The Gospel beyond the West.* Grand Rapids, MI: Eerdmans, 2003.

Seibert, Eric. *The Violence of Scripture: Overcoming the Old Testament's Troubling Legacy.* Minneapolis: Fortress Press, 2012.

Smith, Jamie K. A. *Desiring the Kingdom: Worship, Worldview, and Cultural Formation.* Grand Rapids, MI: Baker Academic, 2009.

Thiessen Nation, Mark, Anthony G. Siegrist, and Daniel P. Umbel. *Bonhoeffer the Assassin? Challenging a Myth, Recovering His Call to Peacemaking.* Grand Rapids, MI: Baker Academic, 2013.

Thomas Aquinas. *Summa theologica.* New York: Benzinger, 1948.

Trible, Phyllis. *Texts of Terror: Literary-Feminist Readings of Biblical Narratives.* Philadelphia: Fortress Press, 1984.

Volf, Miroslav. *A Public Faith: How Followers of Christ Should Serve the Common Good.* Grand Rapids, MI: Brazos Press, 2011.

Weaver, J. Denny. *The Nonviolent Atonement.* Grand Rapids, MI: Eerdmans, 2001.

Wittgenstein, Ludwig. *Philosophical Investigations.* Translated by G. E. M. Anscombe. New York: Macmillan, 1953.

Woodley, Randy. *Shalom and the Community of Creation: An Indigenous Vision.* Grand Rapids, MI: Eerdmans, 2012.

Woolman, John. *The Journal of John Woolman.* Secaucus, NJ: Citadel Press, 1975.

INDEX

THE AUTHOR

Anthony G. Siegrist is a pastor, author, and theologian serving a Mennonite congregation in Ottawa, Ontario. He has advanced degrees from Wycliffe College in the University of Toronto and Eastern Mennonite University. Siegrist has written or edited three books, and his essays have appeared at Missio Alliance, *Bearings Online*, and Syndicate. He enjoys exploring the green spaces and the museums of the Canadian capital with his wife and three young sons.